Spiritual Warfare

Victory In Spiritual Warfare

Francis Wale Oke

Guildford, Surrey

Copyright © 1996 Francis Wale Oke

Victory Literature Crusade
25 Belmont Avenue
Tottenham, London, N17 6AX

Akunleyan Estate
Opposite Green Spring Hotel
Old-Ife Road
P.O. Box 6308, Agodi P.O.
Ibadan – Nigeria

The right of Francis Wale Oke to be identified as author of this work has been asserted by him in accordance with the Copyright, Design and Patents Act 1988.

British Library Cataloguing in Publication Data. A catalogue record for this book is available from the British Library.

Published by Eagle, an imprint of Inter Publishing Service (IPS) Ltd, St Nicholas House, 14 The Mount, Guildford, Surrey GU2 5HN.

All rights reserved. No part of this publication may be reproduced or transmitted in any form or by any means, electronic or mechanical, including photocopying, recording or any information storage and retrieval system, without either prior permission in writing from the publisher or a licence permitting restricted copying.

In the United Kingdom such licences are issued by the Publishers Licensing Society Ltd, 90 Tottenham Court Road, London W1P 9HE.

Bible quotes are from the King James Version (Scofield Study Bible © 1967 O.U.P) unless otherwise stated.

Other versions used are as follows:

NKJV: New King James Version, © 1983 Thomas Nelson Inc.

NIV: New International Version, © 1973, 1978, 1984 by the International Bible Society. Used by permission of Hodder & Stoughton, a Division of Hodder Headline.

Typeset by Palimpsest Book Production Limited,
Polmont, Stirlingshire

Printed and bound in Great Britain by
Caledonian International Book Manufacturing Ltd, Glasgow

ISBN No: 0 86347 200 1

Contents

	Foreword	vi
	Preface	1
One	Prepare To Be An Overcomer	4
Two	Your Enemies Identified	10
Three	The Flesh	19
Four	Victory Over The Flesh	28
Five	Abiding In Victory Over The Flesh	41
Six	The World	53
Seven	How The World Affects The Christian	64
Eight	Victory Over The World	75
Nine	Abiding In Victory Over The World	80
Ten	Your Adversary	86
Eleven	The Devil Is Judged	94
Twelve	Why God Still Allows Satan	104
Thirteen	Victory Over The Devil	114
Fourteen	The Overcomers	121
Fifteen	Character Of The Overcomers	126
Sixteen	Being An Overcomer	135
Seventeen	God's Promises To The Overcomers	141
Eighteen	He That Hath An Ear . . .	146

Foreword

Francis Wale Oke is one of that increasing number of younger leaders in the Nigerian church, both men and women, who have a vision for world mission. He leads a strong church in Ibadan, but has a calling to establish and serve churches abroad, particularly in the United Kingdom and the former Soviet Union.

I have had the privilege of serving with him in Nigeria, and benefiting from the enthusiasm and profound teaching he imparts to his flock. I can still hear, in my memory, the great wave of prayer which rolled over the congregation when Francis exhorted them to pray. In Europe, for centuries, we have rung a bell to bring the faithful to prayer. Here, the bell was rung to curtail prayer by these fervent believers! The candle and the bell used to be the primary religious symbols in Europe. In Africa, it is the Bible and the bell, and both are necessary for a minister in such meetings. You can't get anywhere without them! It is this style of praying that lies behind the spiritual warfare this book addresses.

Spiritual warfare was never meant to be a subject for cerebral controversy. It is a call to battle. Starting in Genesis 3, after the fall of man, we hear war declared:

Foreword

> *'I will put enmity between you and the woman, and between your offspring and hers; he will crush your head and you will strike his heel.'*
>
> v. 15 NIV

For the woman, it added war in the pain of childbirth, and for her husband, the fight against the earth to sustain a living. Between the man and his wife, the war of the sexes began. *'Your desire shall be for your husband, and he shall rule over you.'*

Warfare is foretold by God as the consequence of man's rebellion on this earth. This battle continues through the Scriptures until Christ returns in Revelation 19:

> *And I saw heaven opened, and behold, a white horse! Its rider is called faithful and true, and in righteousness he judges and makes war.'*
>
> *'And the armies of heaven, wearing fine linen, white and pure, were following him on white horses.'*
>
> *'Then I saw the beast and the kings of the earth and their armies assembled to make war against the rider on the horse and against his army.*
>
> vv 11, 14, 19

Christian theology is battle theology. Warfare is not smooth and orderly. In the midst of the fight, soldiers will use anything appropriate to gain mastery over the enemy. They would not stop in the middle of a conflict to discuss the legitimacy or the effectiveness of their method. They are mainly concerned with making sure that the enemy is put under their feet. Surely the devil loves the kind of diversion where we never manage to fight because we are preoccupied with discussing how the fighting should be done.

This book, coming out of the experience of battles for God in an area saturated with demonic opposition, deals with the subject from firsthand encounters. It will benefit all of God's people who wish to get behind the Lord '... *who goes forth like a soldier, stirs his fury like a warrior, cries out and shouts aloud, and shows himself mighty against his enemies*'. Isaiah 42:13.

Francis' book will help us in using our aggression against the enemy and not against our fellow believers, as, sadly, so often we do.

There is another important idea contained within the title of this book. We are not only considering warfare, but victory in warfare, or *overcoming* as it is sometimes translated in the New Testament. It is rare to see emphasis in writing or public teaching on overcoming and the overcomers. It is a subject largely lost in current Western church life. For me, overcoming has been, from my earliest years as a Christian, a stimulus to faith, holiness, and continuing in the race set before me, so that I might win the prize. Not that the prize will be something for me to glory in, but it will be a pleasure for the Father to see his son take the award, as I find pleasure in watching my children take their prizes at school. Not everyone who is a believer will gain the prize, although they are offered the faith which could do it. 1 John 5 says,

'*For whatever is born of God overcomes the world. And this is the victory that has overcome the world, our faith.*

  Who is the one who overcomes the world but the one who believes that Jesus is the Son of God?'

v 4–5

Foreword

At first sight this might appear that every believing person automatically will be an overcomer, but the book of Revelation challenges us seven times in the messages to the churches that we should be those who overcome, and by so doing, please God and gain the advantages which he offers to us. The challenges of the book of Revelation are real ones designed to make believers into overcomers.

Paul knew when he faced execution that he had fought the fight, that he had finished the race, and that he had kept the faith, so he had a prize of a crown of righteousness awaiting him. Not every believer is so blessed in achieving such a crown. I would like to be one who did, and I believe Francis' book will help all true believers, but especially those of us in Europe, where passivity – born of strange views of God's kingdom and proud theology – has kept us out of the fight. It has been left to our African brothers, and others, to wake us from our lethargy and call us to rise and follow them to holiness, world evangelisation and the coming kingdom of God, when Satan will be finally overthrown, and we will reign with him forever and ever.

Francis' book will challenge us to win the fight and win the crown.

Preface

In this tail end of the last days, spiritual warfare has become more real than ever before. The enemy is desperate, knowing that his time is very short. But that God has ordained victory for the Church is certain. *'Upon this rock I will build my church;'* Jesus said, *'and the gates of hell shall not prevail against it'* (Matthew 16:18). God's plan for you is to be more than a conqueror in the battle of life.

This book is not just about spiritual warfare. It speaks of *our victory* that Jesus purchased with His precious blood on the cross at Calvary, and how you can enjoy the fruit of it in your daily life.

The enemies we contend with are exposed, as are the ways they affect our lives. The weapons of our warfare are touched on and how we can skilfully use them to our advantage.

The latter part of the book talks of the overcomers, their characteristics, their conflicts and their victories. The wonderful promises given to those who overcome, by our Lord Jesus Christ are also explored and explained.

There are many voices clamouring for our attention today. But this is what the Spirit is saying to the churches. God wants the Church to be strong. He wants the saints to be overcomers. He wants His people to be more than conquerors.

Jesus Christ is not coming for a weak, discouraged and defeated set of people begging for deliverance. He is coming for a people that are holy and pure, strong and energetic, daring and bold, who are making demons submit and the world tremble because Jesus Christ is Lord. You can be in that company.

I hope you will find in this book a direct message to your heart.

Mr Andrew Bolton, a British solicitor and friend, was giving me a ride to the station in his car the other day when he said to me, 'I read your book *Victory In Spiritual Warfare*. May I say that it is of practical significance and very true to life. It speaks to my situation directly. And it is so solidly anchored on the Scriptures, one cannot argue against the fact that its message is true.' I asked if I could quote him in the preface to the new edition. Though he was surprised at the request, he consented. Andrew is one of the numerous people God used the first edition of this book to bless. If the Lord used the book to bless Andrew, He will use it to bless you.

May I thank Rev Kola Enietan and Mr Tunde Ojo who edited the original manuscript in 1982. Incidentally, it was Rev Enietan again who edited the final work in 1993. I am grateful to God for the lives of Pastor E.A. Adeboye and Rev Wynne Lewis whose valuable friendship have been a blessing to me over the years. Also, Messrs Ed Harding and David Wavre who gave much encouragement on my writing ministry. Lastly, to Colin Urquhart whom God used to make it possible for my works to be published in Great Britain, and subsequently around the world.

I commend this work to the hands of the Holy Spirit,

to use it to liberate people from every form of bondage, that they may enjoy the victory that Jesus Christ purchased for us with His precious blood, to the glory of God our Father.

>   Jesus is Lord.

Francis Wale Oke
Ibadan, 1995

Chapter One

Prepare To Be An Overcomer

God's plan is that everyone of His children should be an overcomer. The Bible is very clear about this.

For whatsoever is born of God overcometh . . .
1 John 5:4

At the moment of conversion, the very life and nature of God is imparted to us as we receive Jesus Christ by faith and are washed in His precious blood. If you are truly a believer in Christ Jesus, then you are a partaker of the divine nature. When you received Jesus Christ as your Saviour and Lord, not only were you forgiven and cleansed from all your sins, you actually received *zoe* – eternal life, the very life of God. That is what the Bible means by being *'born again'*. It is not just 'getting religious'. You become a new creature in Christ Jesus. You may not feel it but that is what it is. It is not by feelings but by faith. That this is true is made very plain in the Bible – the Word of God.

Therefore, if any man be in Christ, he is a new creation; old things are passed away; behold, all things are become new. 2 *Corinthians 5:17*

Prepare To Be An Overcomer

> *Whosoever believeth in him [Christ Jesus] should not perish, but have everlasting life.* John 3:16b
>
> *He has given us his very great and precious promises, so that through them you may participate in the divine nature and escape the corruption in the world caused by evil desires.* 2 Peter 1:4 NIV
>
> *For by grace are ye saved through faith.*
> Ephesians 2:8
>
> *For we walk by faith, not by sight.*
> 2 Corinthians 5:7

That you partake of God's divine nature simply means you have within you God's ability to be an overcomer in life. All you need to do is to take advantage of God's grace in your life and begin to live in high victory. You can do all things through Christ who lives within you. This is not all. God has put His Holy Spirit in us to lead us in constant victory. He has also put His angels on assignment on our behalf to keep us in all our ways lest we dash our feet against the stones (Psalm 91:10–12). He Himself watches over us in all our ways, and He has promised never to leave or forsake us. God has done all He needed to do to ensure that we walk in victory every day of our lives.

Therefore, beloved, if you are indeed a Christian, truly born again, and washed in the precious blood of Jesus Christ, then you are born to reign: you are born to win: you are born to be more than a conqueror. God's nature is in you. The very life of God is in you. The Spirit of God is in you. You are to reign in life through Christ Jesus.

It was on the cross of Calvary where Jesus defeated the devil that your victory was settled for ever. Satan his cohorts are eternally defeated. Jesus is Lord for evermore. And if you have put your trust in His sacrifice at Calvary, you are to walk in the victory that was secured for you there, all the days of your life.

> *For if, by the trespass of the one man, death reigned through that one man, how much more will those who receive God's abundant provision of grace and of the gift of righteousness reign in life through the one man, Jesus Christ.* Romans 5:17 NIV

To be an overcomer is to prevail over our enemies and all negative circumstances, and still stay true to God, strong in His grace and power. Then we can serve God without fear, in holiness and righteousness all the days of our lives. This is the will of God for us.

Many times when we fail and fall, we blame God. This is wrong. If ever there is a problem or failure, the fault is not God's. He has made available all grace to keep us victorious at all times. When His people are taken captive or defeated, there is always a reason for it. I read a scripture recently that set me thinking.

> *Judah was exiled to Babylon **because** the people worshipped idols.*
> 1 Chronicles 9:1 LB (emphasis mine)

The pattern is always the same. Judah will never go into captivity when the people are walking in the light of the Word of God and in intimate fellowship with Yahweh – the God of Israel; but when they go into sin and idolatry and refuse to repent, they get whipped. If you fail at all, don't blame God.

Spiritual Warfare

Being an overcomer implies that there is something to overcome. It gives an impression that there is a war and an enemy. This is very true.

We are engaged in spiritual warfare against the devil and his host of demons who constantly seek to break our fellowship with God, to hinder our spiritual progress and render us useless in the service of the Lord. We must understand this. We should not be ignorant of the devices of the devil.

> *For we wrestle not against flesh and blood, but against principalities, against powers, against the rulers of the darkness of this world, against spiritual wickedness in high places.* Ephesians 6:12

These wicked spirits use all sorts of devices against us. These range from discouragements to disappointments, bereavements, persecutions, hardships, victimisations, family crises, various pressures and difficulties – either at home, at work, at school, in the church, or in society.

They tempt us to sin against God and some of these temptations are cunningly devised.

They could also try to use wrong or unbalanced teachings to confuse, hinder, disturb, weaken and poison us spiritually. Strained relationships, false accusations, emotional stress, strife, fear and discouragement are part of their tools of attack against the saints.

They want to do all they can to defeat us. But in all this, God's plan is for us to overcome and to be more than conquerors. He wants us to win this battle of life every time, and He has done all things to make this possible. Ours is to understand His plan and stay in it; understand what the Word of God says and act on it, and then we shall experience clear victory in every facet of our lives, even under the most trying circumstances.

As we move towards the close of this age, prepare to be and live like an overcomer. Prepare to master the circumstances that face you in life. Prepare to let the devil know that Jesus is Lord and that you are a partaker of the divine nature.

Prepare to prove that God's work of grace in your life is a reality. Prepare to demonstrate that the Word of God is true, that the hosts of hell have been truly defeated at Calvary, that you know where you stand in the grace of God, that indeed you are more than a conqueror.

> *Nay, in all these things we are more than conquerors through him that loved us.* Romans 8:37

Do not think it will be all that smooth. Jesus never said it would be. Rather He said: *'In the world you will have tribulation; but be of good cheer, I have overcome the world'* John 16:33 NKJV. The apostles never said it would be easy. They said: *'we must go through many hardships to enter the kingdom of God'* Acts 14:22 NIV.

Hence, do not think you will not have any trouble with the devil. As a matter of fact, you should prepare to give the devil real trouble, as you fight the good fight of faith.

However, beloved, there is provision in the plan and purpose of God for you to be an overcomer and experience victory in every part of your life – your family, your work, your study, your healing and health, your finances, your business and in your spiritual life.

Prepare To Be An Overcomer

God's earnest desire for you is expressed like this:

Beloved, I wish above all things that thou mayest prosper and be in health, even as thy soul prospereth.   3 John 2

Spiritual prosperity and victory are promised here, '... *as thy soul prospereth*'. Healing and health are included '... *and be in health*'. And there is material and physical prosperity in all you do. This is the wish of God for you *'above all things'*.

It is God's plan for you to overcome, not only for a period of time but throughout your entire life. Then you shall see Jesus face to face and reign with Him as an overcomer for ever in the land of endless day where there is no night.

To him that overcometh will I grant to sit with me in my throne, even as I also overcame, and am set down with my Father in his throne.

        Revelation 3:21

Chapter Two

Your Enemies Identified

There are three major enemies that will want to stand between you and your victory.

These enemies constantly make efforts to see that we fall short of the will and purpose of God, thereby losing our inheritance. They are real enemies that wage war against us and must be taken seriously.

When two boxers get into the ring for a championship fight, they do not joke with one another. Each is desperate for victory. They look for areas where the opponent is vulnerable and hit him there, if possible knocking him out. What happens in the natural is only a shadow of spiritual reality. That is why the Bible says we should *'Fight the good fight of faith'* 1 Timothy 6:12.

The first and nearest enemy is **the flesh**. By this we mean the weakness of the flesh, the sinful passion and the selfish desires of the soul as opposed to the righteousness of God. This will be fully explained in the next few chapters.

The second major enemy is **the world**. When the Bible talks of 'the world', it may mean the earth and all it contains, it may mean a span of time otherwise known as an 'age'. But often it means the systems of this world, the people and their manner of life, the social order of this present age, its attractions and glamours.

Your Enemies Identified

The third enemy is **the devil**. The devil is behind all the troubles and calamities in the world today. Many people know this but they do not know how to overcome him, his hosts and all their devices. God has ordained for you to overcome, and He has provided adequate means. Hence you are well able to overcome this adversary whenever he assaults, and to ultimately prevail against him.

The Origin of Satan

Many people think the devil is an impersonal force or a mere influence. Others think he does not even exist, that the idea of the devil is the product of human imaginations. Nothing can be further from the truth.

The Bible teaches about the existence of the devil as a personality – a personal spiritual being, an angel. He was created by God, not as the devil but as the angel known as Lucifer. He was created a powerful, beautiful archangel of God, occupying the number one position in the rank of angels. But when pride entered into him, he rebelled against God's authority. God then judged him and he became a fallen angel – the devil, Satan.

There are two Bible passages where we are given a glimpse into the origin and the fall of Satan. Let us consider one of them here now.

How art thou fallen from heaven, O Lucifer, son of the morning! How art thou cut down to the ground, who didst weaken the nations!

For thou hast said in thine heart, I will ascend into heaven, I will exalt my throne above the stars of God; I will sit also upon the mount of the congregation, in the sides of the north,

> *I will ascend above the heights of the clouds, I will be like the Most High.*
>
> *Yet thou shalt be brought down to hell, to the sides of the pit.*
>
> *They that see thee shall narrowly look upon thee, and consider thee, saying, Is this the man who made the earth to tremble, who did shake kingdoms,*
>
> *Who made the world like a wilderness, and destroyed its cities, who opened not the house of his prisoners?* Isaiah 14:12–17

Certain facts emerge from this passage of the Scriptures:

First, the devil is a fallen angel. He has fallen from heaven and is under divine judgment. This agrees with the words of our Lord Jesus Christ. *'I saw Satan fall like lightning from heaven'* Luke 10:18 NKJV.

The good angels that still retain their original estate are ministering spirits who are sent by God to minister to us – the heirs of God's salvation (Hebrews 1:14). If the holy angels that have not fallen are to serve us, where then does a fallen angel stand? The devil is only an ex-employee of heaven who was fired. You do not need to be afraid of him at all if **you are abiding in Christ and Christ is in you.**

> *Ye are of God, little children, and have overcome them, because greater is he that is in you, than he that is in the world.* 1 John 4:4

Secondly, Satan fell because pride entered into him. It all began in his heart. He said in his heart 'I will . . . I will . . . , I will . . . , I will . . . , I will . . .' Five times within a short passage, Satan said 'I will'.

Your Enemies Identified 13

The height of his pride was expressed in the words 'I will be like the Most High'! He was so full of himself. He was gunning for the seat of God Almighty. He wanted to be worshipped. He felt God should not be the only one to be worshipped, he must receive attention too. This is the core of Satan-worship, occultism, idolatry and paganism. Satan simply wants to be worshipped. He wants to be God.

People who get involved in any shade or form of Satan-worship and idolatry simply set them against the Almighty God and open their lives for satanic affliction and bondage. Such people need not only to be born again, but also to be delivered from demonic bondage.

The fall of Satan was caused by his pride. Pride is the expression of the very nature of Satan. No wonder God hates pride so much and sets Himself against the proud. When pride enters into a man Satan has set him up for destruction; it is only a matter of time. Beware of pride. God resists the proud but gives grace to the humble.

But he giveth more grace. Wherefore he saith, God resisteth the proud, but giveth grace unto the humble.

Submit yourselves, therefore, to God. Resist the devil, and he will flee from you.   James 4:6–7

To get a clear picture of God's devastating judgment on pride, we need only see the position Satan occupied before his fall. Let us now examine the other scripture that sheds light on the fall of Satan.

Moreover, the word of the LORD came unto me, saying,

> *Son of man, take up a lamentation upon the king of Tyre, and say unto him, Thus saith the LORD GOD; Thou sealest up the sum, full of wisdom, and perfect in beauty.*
>
> *Thou hast been in Eden, the garden of God; every precious stone was thy covering, the sardius, topaz, and the diamond, the beryl, the onyx, and the jasper, the sapphire, the emerald, and the carbuncle, and gold; the workmanship of thy tabrets and of thy pipes was prepared in thee in the day that thou wast created.*
>
> *Thou art the anointed cherub that covereth, and I have set thee so; thou wast upon the holy mountain of God; thou hast walked up and down in the midst of the stones of fire.*
>
> *Thou wast perfect in thy ways from the day that thou wast created, till iniquity was found in thee.*
>
> Ezekiel 28:11–15

From these scriptures, certain things become clear about Satan. God made him perfect, and gave him abundant wisdom and beauty. It appears he was the anointed cherub that was covering the throne of God. He walked up and down in the midst of fire and was probably the musical director of heaven's music. No other angel was quite that close to God. None other was that privileged.

Satan was actually *'perfect in his ways'* until he opened his heart to iniquity and pride. Then he fell. But we see from these scriptures that Satan was created by God and made to be all he was by God.

> *The workmanship of thy tabrets and of thy pipes was prepared in thee in the day that thou wast created.* v 13

Your Enemies Identified

> *Thou art the anointed cherub that covereth; and I have set thee so.* v 14
>
> *Thou wast perfect in thy ways from the day that thou wast created, till iniquity was found in thee.* v 15

This speaks of Satan's limitations. He is not God, he is a creature. The creature can never be stronger or wiser than the creator. The creator still holds the destiny of the creature in his hands. Do not worship Satan. Do not fall before him. Do not be afraid of him. Only fear God and let your life be secure in Jesus Christ.

> *Oh, how great is thy goodness, which thou hast laid up for those who fear thee, which thou hast wrought for those who trust in thee before the sons of men!*
>
> *Thou shalt hide them in the secret of thy presence from the pride of man; thou shalt keep them secretly in a pavilion from the strife of tongues.*
>
> Psalm 31:19–20

Never again should you be afraid of Satan. Now you know his origin. Before you finish this book, you will know his end.

Satan Is Judged

One other glorious fact emerges. Immediately Satan fell, God judged him. '*Yet thou shalt be brought down to hell, to the sides of the pit*' Isaiah 14:15. '*Therefore, I will cast thee as profane out of the mountain of God, and I will destroy thee, O covering cherub, from the midst of the stones of fire.*'

Ezekiel 28:16b

Jesus Christ came to execute that judgment on the cross of Calvary. Satan thought he was killing Jesus but he did not know the wisdom of God. He did not understand the divine strategy that it was through death Christ would execute the judgment on Satan and his cohorts. Through death Christ destroyed the one who had the power of death, and brought liberty for us (Hebrews 2:14–15). That was why Jesus made this pronouncement just when He was about to go to the cross:

> *Now is the judgment of this world; now shall the prince of this world be cast out. And I, if I be lifted up from the earth, will draw all men unto me.*
> John 12:31–32

That He did exactly on the cross. Beloved, rejoice! The devil is judged already. If you are in Christ, you are more than a conqueror through the One who died and overcame the devil for you. Alleluia.

God judged Satan and cast him out of heaven. Some angels rebelled with Satan at that time, and they also came under the same judgment. These are the fallen angels, the evil spirits that we have to contend with in spiritual warfare today. But they are a bunch of defeated foes. Jesus won the victory for us on the cross of Calvary.

The Enemy Of Righteousness

Right from the time of his fall, Satan became the enemy of God. He always seeks to thwart God's plans and programmes. He takes special delight in attacking

Your Enemies Identified

mankind because man is the crown of God's creation and the special object of His favour.

That is why he lured Adam and Eve to sin against God so that they incurred God's displeasure and came under Satan's dominion because of their sin.

God made man originally to have dominion over all the works of His hands. He was made in the image of God and crowned with glory and honour, as the Bible puts it in Genesis 1:26–27.

> *What is man, that thou art mindful of him? And the son of man, that thou visitest him?*
>
> *For thou hast made him a little lower than the angels, and hast crowned him with glory and honour.*
>
> *Thou madest him to have dominion over the works of thy hands; thou hast put all things under his feet.* Psalm 8:4–6

Satan could not exercise any right, authority or dominion over man. Not in the least. But then he came with his temptation, Man listened to the devil and tragedy struck. You remember the Bible says 'know ye not that to whom ye yield yourselves servants to obey, his servants ye are to whom ye obey'. Romans 6:16.

Man then became the devil's servant. Right from that time the devil had rights over man to cause him to sin, to afflict and torment him. But thanks be to God for Jesus Christ who came to deliver us from the bondage of Satan. He met the devil and defeated him at all points so that He might become the Lord of all. And now if you have accepted Jesus as your personal Lord and Saviour, you are delivered from the dominion of the devil, redeemed unto God, and made free indeed. *'If the Son [Jesus], therefore, shall make you free, ye shall be free indeed'* John 8:36.

Satan fell from his exalted position because of pride. Likewise anybody can fall, and stumble and crumble through pride, for *'pride goeth before destruction'*. God hates pride and resists the proud (Proverbs 16:18).

Satan came under God's judgment when he fell into sin – anyone living in sin is under God's judgment. But there is deliverance from every form of judgment through Christ Jesus for anyone who will ask Him for cleansing with His precious blood.

I have dealt extensively with what the Bible says about Satan. More shall be said later in the book. This is not to focus on the enemy as it were, but to give us a clear understanding of what God's Word says about him. There are two attitudes to the enemy that are perilous. We must not overestimate him but at the same time, we must not underestimate him. Every nation knows that before you can effectively fight another nation, you must have a correct assessment of what they have and what they are capable of doing. God warns us not to be ignorant of the devices of the devil.

In summary, there are three enemies we contend against – the flesh, the world, Satan and his hosts. But in all of these, we are more than conquerors through Christ Jesus.

Chapter Three
The Flesh

I have tried to give a definition of 'the flesh'. It can manifest itself in its inherent weakness and inability to do the will of God and its constant resistance against your spirit that is ever seeking to do the will of God.

Resistance

How many times do you actually desire to fast, pray, witness, preach or do one good thing or another that the flesh resists and drags you down?

Deep down within you, you really wanted to do these things, but the flesh said no. This is what the Bible means in this verse:

> *For the flesh lusteth against the Spirit, and the Spirit against the flesh; and these are contrary the one to the other, so that ye cannot do the things that ye would.*   Galatians 5:17

The flesh always rises against us in doing the will of God. Anyone under the dominion of the flesh will yield to it and will not do what God wants him to do. This is the problem with many Christians. Perhaps this is why you are not as prayerful, fruitful, holy and effective as you desire to be in your Christian life.

Paul the apostle had this conflict. Before the Lord gave him a breakthrough he was constantly frustrated in his efforts to please God. He struggled so hard but found that his struggles were futile. Hear what he said:

> *I do not understand what I do. For what I want to do I do not do, but what I hate I do.*
> Romans 7:15 NIV

I am sure we can identify with that. What he did not want to do he was doing. What he wanted to do he could not. That is the work of the flesh.

> *For I know that in me (that is in my flesh) dwelleth no good thing; for to will is present with me, but how to perform that which is good I find not.*
> *For the good that I would, I do not; but the evil which I would not, that I do.* Romans 7:18,19

All along Paul was yearning for liberty. We are not made for bondage, you see. Deep down inside every one of us is a desire to be totally free from all that holds us down. God put that desire there because He wants us to be free.

In desperation, Paul cried out! He could not bear the burden of fleshly bondage anymore.

> *O, wretched man that I am! Who shall deliver me from the body of this death?* Romans 7:24

The Flesh

At this point God took over in the life of Paul. His struggles ceased. He experienced the total victory that Jesus brought for us. He entered into the rest that God has prepared for His people. Relieved, he heaved a sigh and gave glory to Jesus for his liberty. *'I thank God through Jesus Christ, our Lord'* Romans 7:25.

The Lord wants you to overcome in this area and be a master of your body and flesh rather than it being your lord. You will have to obtain your total victory from our Lord Jesus like Paul did. You will have to learn to say 'No' to the flesh whenever it resists doing the will of God and go ahead by faith to do it.

Paul was free from condemnation and guilt. He was free from the burden of the flesh. He could then serve the Lord in liberty, in freedom, with joy and gladness. The spoiler of his joy has been taken out of the way. The law of the Spirit of life in Christ Jesus had made him free from the law of sin and death.

> *For the law of the Spirit of life in Christ Jesus hath made me free from the law of sin and death.*
> Romans 8:2

The Works Of The Flesh

The second way in which the flesh manifests itself is in its inordinate affections, the evil desires and selfish wishes that are quite opposed to the will of God.

In the first instance, the flesh hinders you from doing what God wants you to do, in this case it moves you to do what God says you should not do. This is what the Bible calls the works of the flesh.

The flesh being alive, is why lusts, impure thoughts,

wicked imaginations, lying and deceit, covetousness and greed, gluttony, drunkenness and lack of self-control still are manifest in many people. An unforgiving spirit, pride, cheating of all forms and all manner of immoralities are works of the flesh.

The Bible speaks clearly about this and says that the people who indulge in them cannot inherit the Kingdom of God.

> *Now the works of the flesh are evident, which are: adultery, fornication, uncleanness, lewdness, idolatry, sorcery, hatred, contentions, jealousies, outbursts of wrath, selfish ambitions, dissensions, heresies, envy, murders, drunkenness, revelries and the like;* ***of which I tell you beforehand, just as I also told you in time past, that those who practise such things will not inherit the kingdom of God****.*
> Galatians 5:19–21 NKJV (emphasis mine)

This is one of the major reasons we must seek for and obtain our total victory over the works of the flesh – to inherit the Kingdom of God.

God does not play with His Word. When He says that people who do such things shall not enter into the Kingdom, that is it. Exactly.

Some people in the time of Paul thought that such scriptures addressed others, but that God was going to spare them even though they indulged in the works of the flesh. To such people, Paul warned.

> *But fornication, and all uncleanness or covetousness, let it not even be named among you, as is fitting for saints;*

The Flesh

neither filthiness, nor foolish talking, nor coarse jesting, which are not fitting, but rather giving of thanks.

For this you know, that no fornicator, unclean person, nor covetous man, who is an idolater, has any inheritance in the kingdom of Christ and God.

LET NO ONE DECEIVE YOU WITH EMPTY WORDS, FOR BECAUSE OF THESE THINGS THE WRATH OF GOD COMES UPON THE SONS OF DISOBEDIENCE.

Therefore do not be partakers with them.
    Ephesians 5:3–7 NKJV (emphasis mine)

Some people tend to ignore such clear warnings, and teachings and encouragements of the Scriptures. They reason that we cannot have victory over the works of the flesh while we are still alive. This is a deceit of the enemy to keep people in bondage. What God has said in His Word is very true. He can give total victory over all the works of the flesh and help you not to lose your inheritance in His Kingdom like Esau.

Esau had all the opportunities. He was the first-born and the inheritance belonged to him automatically. But by indulging the flesh he lost it. For a momentary passing pleasure, he lost his eternal inheritance. Later in life he sought it carefully with tears but it was too late. This is why the Bible warns

Lest there be any fornicator, or profane person, like Esau, who for one morsel of meat sold his birthright.

For ye know how that afterward, when he would have inherited the blessing, he was rejected; for he found no place of repentance, though he sought it carefully with tears.   Hebrews 12:16–17

There are many believers who would have been mighty instruments in the hands of God but missed it because they indulged in the works of the flesh and they are not prepared to truly repent. Many people shall miss the glory of heaven simply because of this.

This is a clear warning to all of us. God is calling His people to repentance, that we may enter into our inheritance and fulfil His divine purpose for our lives.

God wants to lead us and be our Shepherd. He does not simply want to bless our programmes and plans merely because we have presented them to Him. He wants us to find out His will and His ways for our lives. The flesh however, always wants to seek its own way, whether or not it is God's will. Of course the way of the flesh is never the way of God.

This is a battle every Christian must win. Our greatest desire should be to do the will of God from the heart. It should go beyond the level of desire. We should be committed to doing God's will at all times. And we should be prepared to pay whatever price is required in order to finish the flesh and all its works in our lives and then move on to fulfil God's plan and purpose.

Satan will try to deceive us into thinking the will of God is difficult, frustrating and boring. He will then bring his alternatives that look attractive, glamorous and exciting. But remember, Satan's apples are full of worms. Oh! there is great joy and peace doing the will of God. Nothing can be as truly exciting and fulfilling as walking in the perfect will of God for your life. When you remember that God is your Father, that He loves you dearly and is committed to your joy and welfare, you will reject Satan's alternatives and joyfully walk in the will of God your Father.

Rebelliousness

The third way the flesh manifests itself is in its desire and effort to do its wishes rather than the perfect will of God. It always seeks to avoid the way of the cross, wanting rather the easier way out.

Certain things are not sinful in themselves: but they are not edifying. The flesh will want to find excuses to indulge in them. The Bible says:

> *All things are lawful unto me, but all things are not expedient; all things are lawful for me, but I will not be brought under the power of any.*
> 1 Corinthians 6:12

Some relationships and associations may not be sinful but at the same time not edifying. Watching the TV for four hours every evening may not be sinful, but certainly there is some Kingdom business you could be profitably engaged in that will be truly more enriching. What of spending one of those four hours praying daily! There are ways you can spend your money that may not be sinful, but are neither wise nor contribute meaningfully to the Kingdom of God.

The man who is an overcomer will go the extra mile and will not just bury himself in things that do not edify, by convincing himself that they are not necessarily sinful. He will always seek to redeem the time, and live every bit of his life to the glory of God.

Many a time, we decide on what we want to do without caring whether or not it is the perfect will of God. This again is the flesh at work. There are those who act presumptuously doing things God has not asked them to do. Uncommanded assignment! This is the flesh at work. The Lord wants to be our

Shepherd and lead us in His way. He knows what is best. He knows the way through the wilderness. All we have to do is to follow. To be victorious over the flesh, let Jesus truly be your Shepherd. Rather than going into a venture and then asking for His blessing, you ask for His perfect will and let Him lead you into it. Many times He leads us through the way of the cross. Tough, demanding, sacrificial and contrary to your expectations. Naturally the flesh recoils and withdraws. The flesh *never* loves the way of the cross because it means death to the flesh. But without the cross there is no resurrection. Before we can truly live in the newness of life we have to pass through the gateway of the cross. And please remember, God is only using the cross to bring out the best in us.

The Abominations Of The Flesh

Before we go on to show how a believer can live in constant victory over the flesh, note that the works of the flesh, no matter how little, are an abomination before the Lord. Those who walk in the flesh, obeying the lust of it cannot walk and live by faith. They cannot please God. This is frightening, but that is the truth.

They that are in the flesh cannot please God.
Romans 8:8

The flesh is an enemy of God. It violently resists the will of God. Hence if you yield to the flesh you are taking sides with the enemy of God.

Because the carnal mind [the flesh] is enmity against God; for it is not subject to the law of God, neither, indeed, can be. Romans 8:7

The Flesh

To walk in the flesh is to be carnal-minded. It is to always desire the evil passion of the flesh and walk in sin. Walking in the flesh brings sorrow, disturbs your peace with God, breaks your fellowship with Him, robs you of His rich blessings and renders you useless in the hands of God.

Finally the flesh leads to death if it is not crucified on time.

For to be carnally minded is death, but to be spiritually minded is life and peace. Romans 8:6

Now think over your spiritual life. Think of the various conflicts you have had. Think of the many times the flesh has defeated you. You should obtain your victory over this deadly enemy of your soul and begin to walk in victory.

Many appear to be giants elsewhere; in preaching, in praying, in counselling and many other areas, but before this enemy they constantly fall flat. Now your victory is here – through the Lord Jesus Christ. He wants to make you free from the flesh and all its ugly works. Trust Him to do it, now.

If the Son, therefore, shall make you free, ye shall be free indeed. John 8:36

Chapter Four

Victory Over The Flesh

The Bible says that the flesh or the carnal mind is not obedient to the will of God, and cannot possibly be. This is terrifying.

Because the carnal mind is enmity against God: for it is not subject to the law of God, neither, indeed, can be.
                                            Romans 8:7

This shows clearly that there is only one way to have victory over the flesh. The flesh must die. There is no other way. You cannot reform the flesh. You cannot educate it. Neither can you refine it. This flesh must be left to die, never to resurrect again.

This sounds drastic, but I am sure you will agree with me that a drastic problem deserves a drastic approach. If the flesh will lead to your death, then let's kill it first. Moreover, it is God's only solution to the problem of the flesh.

Therefore put to death your members which are on the earth: fornication, uncleanness, passion, evil desire, and covetousness, which is idolatry.

Because of these things the wrath of God is coming upon the sons of disobedience, in which you yourselves once walked when you lived in them.
                                    Colossians 3:5–7 NKJV

Victory Over The Flesh

God is saying that we are to put the flesh and all its works to death directly. I know you want to have victory over the flesh. I know you want to live your life to the glory of God. But it will mean death to your flesh. How?

There are two steps to this victory. If you sincerely take them by faith and with firmness of purpose, your victory is as sure as the throne of God.

But before then, let me ask you a most crucial question. Are you born again? Have you repented of your sins? Have you accepted Jesus as your personal Lord and Saviour? If not, do it now, because you cannot overcome the flesh, the world, or the devil unless you have accepted Jesus as your Lord and Saviour.

> *Who can overcome . . . ? Only the man who believes that Jesus is the Son of God.*
> 1 John 5:5 Jerusalem Bible

It is the Lord Jesus living in you that gives you victory over the flesh and all its works. This is your first step to victory. It is so foundational that nothing else works until that is settled.

Dead To Sin

If you are already born again with the Holy Spirit, the witness in you, there is good news for you. You are already dead in Christ Jesus!

We said earlier that the only solution to the flesh is for it to die. You (your flesh) is already dead. You ought to know this as a living reality. Ignorance of this is what the devil uses to stir up the flesh to come alive and trouble you and cause you to stumble from time to time. Recognise this fact: you are already dead to sin, your flesh is already dead in Christ. Where and when did it happen? On the cross, when and where Jesus died. There and then you died with Him! This is the truth. The enemy wants to hide this from us, or keep us from believing it because he knows it is crucial to our victory. But hear what the Bible says.

> *Knowing this, that our old man is crucified with him, that the body of sin might be destroyed, that henceforth we should not serve sin.* Romans 6:6

This 'old man' is the flesh. It gives inspiration to your body to commit sin, to become a tool of sin. It is referred to as the body of sin. But the old man is crucified with Christ so that the body might be rendered powerless as far as sin is concerned. You should absorb that and confess it to yourself again and again until it becomes a part of your being.

In Colossians the Bible says *'For ye are dead, and your life is hidden with Christ in God'* Colossians 3:3. This is to say that as far as sin is concerned, and the lusts of the flesh, you are dead. But you are alive to righteousness in Christ Jesus the Lord. If you are not convinced about this, please check up Romans 6:3–4. *'Know ye not that, as many of us as were baptised into Jesus Christ were baptised into his death? Therefore we are buried with him by baptism into death.'* This is not just talking of water baptism. In water baptism you are giving a physical witness to a spiritual reality that has taken place in your life. As you are buried in water, you are testifying that in receiving Jesus as your Saviour and Lord, you have been baptised or buried into Christ,

Victory Over The Flesh

that you have identified completely with His death. As you emerge from the water of baptism you testify that you have identified with the glorious resurrection of Jesus from the dead, and that you now have a brand new, victorious life in Christ.

It means you are to live as someone who is indeed dead to sin. A dead man does not give any response. He is dead. He does not feel anything. This should be your attitude to sin because you are dead to it already in Christ Jesus. You are to live and walk in holiness and purity.

If you poke a dead man with a six-inch nail, what is his reaction? There is the body of a man lying on the floor and you put a bag of cement upon his chest, does he cry out, 'Hey there, what are you doing to me?' Not in the least. He is dead so he cannot respond to any external stimuli. Likewise you. You are dead in Christ. Dead to sin and unrighteousness. That is what Jesus did for us on the cross. We can enjoy total victory over sin and the wishes of the flesh. We can get to a state where even though we are tempted to sin we are not enticed any more. We can walk in absolute victory.

We have just described what the Lord did for us at Calvary. There we were crucified with Christ. We actually died. There is nothing we can do about that. Jesus did it all. Through His death and resurrection, He broke the power of sin and the flesh once and for all.

For what the law could not do, in that it was weak through the flesh, God sending his own son, in the likeness of sinful flesh and for sin, condemned sin in the flesh,

That the righteousness of the law might be fulfilled in us, who walk not after the flesh, but after the Spirit. Romans 8:3–4

In 1992, I was a guest speaker at the combined fellowship of the Full Gospel Businessmen's Fellowship International at Aba, Abia state of Nigeria. There were about 2,000 people present. I heard the testimony of a young man that will remain with me for some time.

He was a murderer. He actually killed someone and was arrested. While he was remanded in prison custody, he heard the Gospel message and was gloriously saved. His conversion was so radical that other inmates took note of it.

When he was to take his plea at the court, the trial judge asked him whether or not he was guilty. 'Yes, my Lord, I am guilty.' Everybody was stunned, including the prosecutor.

The normal thing is for the accused to plead not guilty and then legal battle will ensue. However, the trial went on.

On the day of judgment, it was so clear what the verdict would be. The judge was in red. The accused was brought in handcuffed. The police were fully armed.

'Guilty,' the judge said. 'But before I sentence you, what do you have to say?'

The young man thought to himself, 'No matter what I say I shall be hanged. Why can't I use this opportunity to preach the Gospel to this crowded court.' And that was exactly what he did.

In conclusion, he broke down in tears and said, 'Your honour, the man who was a murderer is dead. The man you are now looking at is a new person. Jesus came into my life while in custody and I am not the same again.' The whole court was completely quiet. Most people had tears in their eyes. This was no drama at all. It was totally unpremeditated. Everyone was at a loss as to what was going to happen.

The judge ordered the court to go on recess. On

Victory Over The Flesh

coming back, the young man was set free. Now he is testifying to the saving grace of Jesus all over Nigeria. His testimony: the man who was a murderer is dead, I am a new person in Christ Jesus. That is the truth and the beauty of the Gospel.

> *What shall we say then? Shall we continue in sin, that grace may abound?*
> *God forbid. How shall we, that are dead to sin, live any longer in it?*
> *Therefore, we are buried with him by baptism into death, that as Christ was raised up from the dead by the glory of the Father, even so we also should walk in newness of life.* Romans 6:1–2, 4

The key issues of the above scripture are worthy of emphasis. We are dead to sin and we cannot live in it any longer. We have been buried with Christ into His death by baptism. As Jesus Christ was raised from the dead by the glory of God the Father, we should walk and live in newness of life.

Understand that at Calvary the power of sin over your life was broken. At Calvary your flesh was crucified with Christ. Therefore, sin should no longer have dominion over you at all. You should overcome sin and the works of the flesh. You do not owe the flesh anything so you should not be under its dominion.

> *For sin shall not have dominion over you; for ye are not under the law but under grace.* Romans 6:14

Meditate on this and confess it to yourself again and again until your faith grasps it. This is the truth that will set you free. Paul the apostle knew this fact well and confessed it boldly. He said he had been crucified with Christ. He said he was living by faith, and victoriously.

And you can repeat this confession of faith and see how the Word of God liberates from the bondage of the flesh.

> *I am crucified with Christ: nevertheless I live; yet not I, but Christ liveth in me; and the life which I now live in the flesh I live by the faith of the Son of God, who loved me and gave himself for me.*
> Galatians 2:20

Jesus has broken the power of sin and its dominion over us. We have no obligation to the flesh. We should not yield to its weaknesses or obey its lusts. Begin to see Christ living in you and begin to live by His faith. You belong to Christ and you should overcome the flesh, because, *'They that are Christ's have crucified the flesh with the affections and lusts'* Galatians 5:24.

Make sure you really grasp this first step to victory. The devil will not want you to understand it. You are crucified with Christ if you have been born again. It is a glorious reality.

What To Do To Overcome The Flesh

The second part is just as important as the first. If it is not taken properly, you may not realise the victory that Jesus has given you over the flesh of sin. The first part speaks of what God has already done for us. There is nothing you can do to it. It is finished. All you have to do is to believe and appropriate it. However, there are certain things you are to do to make this victory

Victory Over The Flesh

God has purchased for you a reality. The Bible is very clear on what your role is. It is twofold.

First, do not yield your body to sin. Do not yield yourself to the cravings and desires of the flesh. Do not allow your body to be used as an instrument of sin.

The devil will surely bring temptations – he will tempt you. But if you do not yield he cannot force you to commit sin. We know very well that we fall into temptation when there is a secret desire, a secret love for the sin and a secret yielding to it right in our hearts. The Bible is very clear on the process of committing sin.

> *Let no man say when he is tempted, I am tempted of God; for God cannot be tempted with evil, neither tempteth he any man;*
> *But every man is tempted, when he is drawn away of his own lust, and enticed.*
> *Then when lust hath conceived, it bringeth forth sin; and sin, when it is finished, bringeth forth death.* James 1:13–15

Did you read that? Every man is tempted when he is drawn away of his own evil desire and enticed.

The devil cannot force you to sin. He only brings the temptations, appealing to you to go into sin. When you agree with the suggestions of the devil and do what he wants, then you sin. But if the tempter comes, and you refuse to yield, victory will come and the devil will be put to shame.

> *Therefore do not let sin reign in your mortal body so that you obey its evil desires.*
> *Do not offer the parts of your body to sin, as instruments of wickedness.* Romans 6:12–13 NIV

Having known that the power and authority of sin have been destroyed over you at Calvary, it is now your duty to refuse to allow sin to reign in your body. It is your duty not to yield to temptation. It is your duty not to allow any part of your body to be used by the devil as an instrument of sin.

As you sincerely and constantly refuse to allow sin to reign in your body, the victory Christ has given you over the flesh will become real. This is the lifestyle of God's overcomers. They refuse to allow the enemy to drag them into sin. They have made up their minds that by saying a decisive 'No' to Satan they will live for the glory of God.

And as for the sins and habits you have allowed in the past, sincerely repent of them and forsake them. Put away from you all the works of the flesh – all lying, hypocrisy, malice, bitterness, envy, covetousness, greed, hatred, unforgiving spirit, lust, fornication, adultery and evil thoughts. Put them away from you and start to walk in newness of life.

These are things that are bringing the awful judgment of God upon the world so speedily. Do not say God will spare you because you have been born again. No. He is no respecter of persons. In fact the judgment will begin in His household, among His people. Therefore separate yourself from evil.

This is an area of conflict in spiritual warfare. The devil will want to wage a psychological battle. He wants to hide from you or hinder you from knowing that you are completely identified with Christ in His death. That you are dead to sin and all the works of the flesh. As a man thinks, so he is. If you think you are not dead to sin, you will find your mind is filled with all sorts of thoughts and ideas, pulling you to sin against God.

But beloved, take your stand on the word of the

Scriptures. In reality, if you are truly in Christ, you are dead to sin and the flesh and you are alive unto God. Refuse to yield your body to sin in any form.

> *Put to death, therefore, whatever belongs to your earthly nature: sexual immorality, impurity, lust, evil desires and greed, which is idolatry. Because of these, the wrath of God is coming. You used to walk in these ways, in the life you once lived. But now you must rid yourselves of all such things as these: anger, rage, malice, slander and filthy language from your lips. Do not lie to each other, since you have taken off your old self with its practices and have put on the new self, which is being renewed in knowledge in the image of its Creator.*   Colossians 3:5–10 NIV

Yield Your Body to God

Secondly, you should yield your body and all parts of your being to God to use for His glory. Do not allow the devil to use your body to sin, yield your body totally to God for His glorious use. Yield your entire person. The devil will want to make a cheap bargain with you to give him just 'a little part' and give the rest to God. But do not listen to him. '*A little leaven leaveneth the whole lump*' 1 Corinthians 5:6. Give your entire being to God, wholly for His use.

> *Rather offer yourselves to God, as those who have been brought from death to life; and offer the parts of your body to him as instruments of righteousness.*   Romans 6:13 NIV

> *I beseech you therefore, brethren, by the mercies of God, that ye present your bodies a living sacrifice, holy, acceptable unto God, which is your reasonable service.*
> Romans 12:1

The Bible says when you yield yourself to God completely you are merely doing what you ought to do. It is your *'reasonable service'* (KJV). It is your *'spiritual act of worship'* (NIV). It is what is best for you if you want to enjoy victory in spiritual warfare.

I remember a folk story I was told while in primary school over thirty years ago. It was about a mighty warrior. This man was such an irresistible conqueror, he won every single battle he fought. No matter how many arrows were shot at him, none would penetrate. The story says his mother, when he was young, dedicated him to warfare, demonically. She dipped him in a mystic water, covering his whole body, for protection.

As a result, no arrow or bullet from the enemy would ever be able to penetrate his body. However his mother held him by one foot when she dipped his body in the water. The water covered him completely – except that tiny portion of his foot where his mother held him. He grew up to be a mighty warrior and no one knew how to kill him. But one day, a stray arrow hit him on the foot – the exact place where his mother had held him when dipping him in the water. He bled and died, and that was his end.

The enemy will look for that tiny part of you that is not totally given to the Lord. If there is any, he will use it against you. You must dedicate your entire being to God.

When you yield your whole being to God, the devil has no way of using any part of you. The Lord will possess you by His Spirit and use you for His glory

Victory Over The Flesh

as a vessel unto honour in His hands. You will not only be an overcomer but you will also inspire others to become overcomers.

> *'If any one purifies himself from what is ignoble, then he will be a vessel for noble use, consecrated and useful to the master of the house, ready for any good work'*   2 Timothy 2:21 RSV.

Begin now to yield yourself wholly to God. Begin to say 'No' to the devil and his temptations. Begin to let the fruit of righteousness come forth in your life. Begin to live like an overcomer.

> *'Therefore, as God's chosen people, holy and dearly loved, clothe yourselves with compassion, kindness, humility, gentleness and patience. Bear with each other and forgive whatever grievances you may have against one another. Forgive as the Lord forgave you. And over all these virtues put on love, which binds them all together in perfect unity.*
>   Colossians 3:12–14 NIV

In summary, realise that Jesus has dealt with the power of sin over your life and that you are crucified with Him. You are dead to sin, and alive to God. Jesus has solved the sin problem.

Therefore do not allow sin to reign in your life. Do not yield to temptation and the lusts of the flesh. Do not allow the devil to make use of any part of your body. But rather yield yourself entirely to God and let Him possess you anew. Begin to manifest the virtues and the love of God and let God start to use the whole of your being for His glory.

If you will obey this word of the Lord, and put it into

practice, you will walk in victory over the flesh every day of your life.

If there is one thing you really need, it is abiding victory over sin and the works of the flesh. This is provided for us as children of God. The devil has taken advantage of us long enough: let us begin to possess our possession. We are more than conquerors through Christ Jesus the Lord.

For sin shall not have dominion over you; for ye are not under the law but under grace. Romans 6:14

Chapter Five

Abiding In Victory Over The Flesh

As you prayerfully read through this book the Holy Spirit will open your understanding and use the truth to give you victory. It is the will of God for you to abide in this victory. I therefore want to show you the way you can live in victory and be more than a conqueror.

Victory By The Word

First and foremost to abide in this victory you have to store the Word of God in your heart. By the Word of God I mean the written word as found in the Bible. You are to read it, study it, meditate on it, memorise it and store it in your spirit. *'Let the word of Christ dwell in you richly, in all wisdom teaching and admonishing one another, in psalms and hymns and spiritual songs singing with grace in your hearts to the Lord'* Colossians 3:16.

This is the way to overcome. When you have the Word of God in you, the Spirit of God will inspire you to use this Word against the devil whenever he comes to tempt you, and you will win. It is the Word that the Lord Jesus

Christ Himself used to defeat the devil when He was tempted in the wilderness. If you have the Word of God in you, you will be able to live a pure and holy life.

> *How can a young man cleanse his way?*
> *By taking heed according to Your word.*
> *Your word I have hidden in my heart.*
> *That I might not sin against You.*
>
> Psalm 119:9, 11 NKJV

Many do not take time to study the Word of God. It is the last of their priorities. This is why many do not overcome as they should. I once talked with a brother who had problems in his spiritual life. I tried to counsel him from the Word of God, but I knew I had not found what his problem was. But as we bowed our heads to pray, the Holy Spirit showed me in a flash that his problem was that he was not taking time to meditate in the Word of God. I told him this and he confirmed it. He then went away, took time to study the Word and his whole life began to change for good.

Take time to get into the Word. It is not just reading articles about the Word, or listening to messages about the Word or reading commentaries. We need all these, but stop depending on second-hand feeding, go to the Bible. Pray and ask the Lord to teach you. Begin to study it systematically, and you will grow tremendously.

I had an experience with a brother in 1979 that confirms the vital place of the Word of God in having victory. He was a student at the University of Lagos and I was then the Bible study secretary of the Lagos Varsity Christian Union. He went for end-of-session holidays and due to parental and peer pressures he fell back into sin. On starting back the following

Abiding in Victory Over The Flesh

session, he kept away from the fellowship and avoided me meticulously. But I was after him. After many attempts I got his attention and succeeded in leading him back to the Lord. I then encouraged him to study the Scriptures daily, making sure he was consistent at it. I gave him a watchword: No Bible, No Breakfast. He was faithful, and I checked him regularly.

Within three months of consistently studying the Word, he became so strong in the faith, he had even led others to the Lord. Studying the Scriptures daily became part of his life. And he has been happy ever since. Now he serves as a deacon in a pentecostal church in Lagos.

The Word is the food for your spirit. For your body to be strong and healthy you need to feed it with good and balanced food, regularly. Likewise if your spirit is to be strong for you to be an overcomer you need to feed it with the Word of God regularly and deeply. The Bible says, *'Let the word of Christ dwell in you richly.'* Let it dwell in you in abundance. If the Word dwells in you, your prayer will be answered (John 15:7). You will prosper in all you do (Psalm 1:1–3).

Do not forget, to abide in the victory God has given you, take time to meditate in the Word of God.

A brother once wrote on the inside cover of his Bible: 'This book will keep you from sin or sin will keep you from this book'. It is true. If you bury yourself in sin you will loathe the Word of God. If you bury yourself in the Word you will hate to sin at all.

This book of the law shall not depart out of thy mouth, but thou shalt meditate therein day and night, that thou mayest observe to do according to all that is written therein; for then thou shalt make thy way prosperous, and then thou shalt have good success. Joshua 1:8

No Place To The Devil

Secondly, to abide in this victory you should not allow any place for the devil in your life. He will tempt you from time to time. But do not allow him to lead you to sin. Temptation is no sin. But yielding to it is sin.

You have the life and the ability of God in you to enable you overcome every temptation. It is a shameful thing to allow the devil to overcome you. It is like allowing him to overcome the Lord Jesus who is living in you. Do not give any place for him.

Neither give place to the devil. Ephesians 4:27

Many Christians lead themselves into temptation. They tempt the devil to tempt them. When you see anything that can hinder your spiritual progress, or lead you into sin or draw you back, you are to flee. You don't go along and play with sin.

You do not go along and join up with anyone who will draw you into sin. You do not go along and put your neck into a yoke with unbelievers or hypocrites or people living loose and sinful lifestyles or enter into alliance with them – either in marriage or business or anything that will get you inseparably involved.

Abiding in Victory Over The Flesh

Flee every appearance of sin. You do not touch things that can lead you or others into sin. Anything filthy, anything that will not help your faith grow – flee it. Do not give in to the devil.

There are many who did not heed this biblical warning and they fell. Even people strong in the Lord have fallen because they did not obey the Lord in this area. Take heed and flee. Resist the devil and shun his enticement.

> *Flee fornication, Every sin that a man doeth is without [outside] the body; but he that committeth fornication sinneth against his own body.*
>
> *What? Know ye not that your body is the temple of the Holy Ghost who is in you, whom ye have of God, and ye are not your own?*
>
> *For ye are bought with a price; therefore, glorify God in your body and in your spirit, which are God's.*   1 Corinthians 6:18–20

> *Abstain from all appearance of evil.*
> 1 Thessalonians 5:22

> *But thou, O man of God, flee these things, and follow after righteousness, godliness, faith, love, patience, meekness.*
>
> *Fight the good fight of faith, lay hold on eternal life, unto which thou art also called and hast professed a good profession before many witnesses.*
> 1 Timothy 6:11–12

> *Now the end of the commandment is charity [love] out of a pure heart and of a good conscience, and of faith unfeigned, from which some, having swerved, have turned aside unto vain jangling.*
> 1 Timothy 1:5–6

> *Holding faith, and a good conscience, which some having put away concerning faith, have made shipwreck.* 1 Timothy 1:19
>
> *Neither give place to the devil.* Ephesians 4:27

Pure And Positive Thought

Thirdly, for you to abide in victory you have to learn to think rightly and positively. There is a great spiritual battle going on in the thought realm and if you are defeated there you will experience defeat in all other areas.

We have to put our thinking right. As a man thinks in his heart so he is, the Bible says. Many are so negative in their thinking and these negative thoughts bring defeat. Thinking about accidents, failures, disappointments, sickness, defeat, grudges, disagreements, will always get you into trouble.

Many of these evil thoughts are demonic in origin and manifestation. I have met people who think evil thoughts and a short while afterward they happened. Recently a lady came to me who needed deliverance. Her mind was always flooded with evil and wicked thoughts – both about herself and other people. And the thoughts always come to pass. She might just be thinking of herself being involved in an accident in which she just managed to escape – and it would happen. She could think about a friend losing a child, and it would happen. She was worried and she came for deliverance. This certainly is not normal.

There was a demonic dimension to the problem. After she told her story, I enquired about her family background. It was then I discovered there was a witchcraft demon at work, which was a common thing

Abiding in Victory Over The Flesh

in her family. We ministered to her, cast the demon out, and she has been free ever since.

To others, it is not wicked thoughts as much as impure, immoral thoughts. Lust, unclean and filthy thoughts fill the hearts of many so that they find it really difficult to live in holiness.

Impure and unclean imaginations are wrong and sinful. Put together, negative and unclean thoughts will always get you into trouble and defile you. The scripture says:

> *Finally, brethren, whatever things are true, whatever things are honest, whatever things are just, whatever things are pure, whatever things are lovely, whatever things are of good report, if there be any virtue, and if there be any praise, think on these things.* Philippians 4:8

These are the things you are to set your thinking upon. You need to store the Word of God in you for you to think right. Whenever you want to think on anything ask yourself these questions: Is it true? Is it honest? Is it just? Is it pure? Is it lovely? Is it of good report? Is it virtuous? Is it praiseworthy for me to think on this? If it does not pass these tests forget it. Start to think right.

If any wrong thought or imagination hangs around your mind, against your will, God has provided you with weapons to deal with it. Use the name of Jesus and the Word of God to cast such imaginations down and bring the thought to the obedience of Christ.

> *For the weapons of our warfare are not carnal, but mighty through God to the pulling down of strong holds*

> *Casting down imaginations, and every high thing that exalteth itself against the knowledge of God, and bringing into captivity every thought to the obedience of Christ.* 2 Corinthians 10:4–5

Learn to think positively. Learn to think right.

Give Yourself To Prayer

Lastly, to abide in victory, you have to give yourself continuously to prayer. The Lord Jesus Christ knows the danger the flesh poses. He urged us to watch and pray.

> *Watch ye and pray, lest ye enter into temptation. The spirit truly is ready, but the flesh is weak.*
> Mark 14:38

Many have taken this verse to excuse the flesh and indulge in its works. The Lord gave this as an antidote against the lusts of the flesh. He told us to watch and pray so that our willing spirit may overcome the unwilling flesh. You need to be prayerful and watchful to abide in victory over the flesh. It is as you pray that you build up your spirit to overcome the drag of the flesh. You can enjoy victory at all times as you take time to pray.

> *But ye, beloved, building up yourselves on your most holy faith, praying in the Holy Ghost.* Jude 20

It is very important for you to watch and pray and to overcome the flesh at this time. It is crucial. The end of all things is at hand. The coming of the Lord Jesus is very near. Let this be real to you. Be ready always to meet the Lord in the air. And you can be ready by being watchful and prayerful.

> *But the end of all things is at hand; be ye, therefore, sober, and watch unto prayer.*   1 Peter 4:7

In The Company Of The Overcomers

The Bible gives a clear indication that not all who call Jesus their Lord will overcome and enter into glory. Hence the various warnings. It is good for you to heed these and be ready to meet the Lord and join the company of the overcomers.

These warnings in the Scriptures are not given to scare or threaten us. No. To be forewarned, people say, is to be forearmed. God sent these words to us to let us know that each of us has to qualify to be called an overcomer. No cross, no crown, goes the old adage. *'If we suffer, we shall also reign with him'* 2 Timothy 2:12.

We must take advantage of God's means of grace and assume full responsibility for the way we live our Christian lives.

> *Watch ye, therefore, and pray always, that ye may be accounted worthy to escape all these things that shall come to pass, and to stand before the Son of man.*   Luke 21:36

> *Watch ye, therefore; for ye know not when the master of the house cometh, at even, or at midnight, or at the cockcrowing, or in the morning.*
> *Lest coming suddenly, he find you sleeping.*
> *And what I say unto you I say unto all, Watch*   Mark 13:35–37

Sometime ago, as I was meditating on a portion of the scripture describing the overcomers, I saw clearly that before they could be regarded as overcomers, they overcame the flesh and all its lusts and all its affections. This is an area of battle that has to be taken more seriously than ever before. You must have your victory over the flesh and all of its works if you will reign with Christ.

> *And I looked, and, lo, a Lamb stood on Mount Zion, and with him an hundred forty and four thousand, having his Father's name written in their foreheads.* Revelation 14:1

The overcomers will have the Father's name written on their forehead, not the mark of the beast or the anti-Christ.

> *And I heard a voice from heaven, like the voice of many waters, and like the voice of a great thunder; and I heard the voice of harpers harping with their harps.* Revelation 14:2

There will be so much joy and celebration when we get to glory. The overcomers shall rejoice and jubilate forever.

> *And they sang, as it were, a new song before the throne, and before the four beasts and the elders; and no man could learn that song but the hundred and forty and four thousand, who were redeemed from the earth.* Revelation 14:3

There are blessings exclusively reserved for the overcomers. It is not everyone in the Church that will

Abiding in Victory Over The Flesh

qualify. Make up your mind to be in the overcomers' band.

> *These are they who were not defiled with women; for they are virgins. These are they who follow the Lamb wherever he goeth. These were redeemed from among men, the firstfruits unto God and to the Lamb.*
> *And in their mouth was found no guile; for they are without fault before the throne of God.*
> Revelation 14:4–5

'[They] were not defiled with women; for they are virgins.' This does not mean they were not married. Marriage is not defilement in any sense if it is within the will of God. As a matter of fact, the Bible says that marriage is honourable and the bed undefiled. It simply means they did not mess around with immorality and lasciviousness. They kept themselves pure from sexual sins and lived a life of holiness unto God.

They also followed the Lamb wherever He went. Their obedience and consecration was complete. They were not half-hearted in their commitment to Christ. Neither were they lukewarm in their devotion to God. They followed Him all the way, loving Him with all their heart, and soul, and mind, and strength.

You should prepare to be in the company of the overcomers. If you are defiled by sin and the works of the flesh, there is provision made for you. You can confess your sins in genuine repentance and believe God to forgive you. Then continue to walk in the victory of Calvary. If you have been walking in this victory, keep on walking steadily and steadfastly and do not give room for the flesh to defile your garment. Very shortly, the Lord Jesus Christ shall come. The saints of the most High shall possess the Kingdom for ever, even for ever and ever.

> *But the saints of the Most High shall take the kingdom, and possess the kingdom for ever, even forever and ever.* Daniel 7:18

We shall be allowed to enter into the everlasting Kingdom of our God and so shall we ever be with the Lord.

> *Behold. I come as a thief. Blessed is he that watcheth, and keepeth his garments, lest he walk naked, and they see his shame.* Revelation 16:15

By the grace of God I shall not be naked and ashamed at the coming of the Lord Jesus Christ. I shall keep my garment unspotted and undefiled. This is the overcomers stand. It should be your stand too.

Chapter Six

The World

The Bible says, *'The earth is the LORD's, and the fulness thereof'* Psalm 24:1. God created the heavens and the earth and everything in them, and He has not gone on vacation, abandoning His creation. Right now Jesus Christ still upholds all things by the Word of His power, and without Him nothing holds together.

> *Who, being the brightness of his glory, and the express image of his person, and upholding all things by the word of his power . . .* Hebrews 1:3

However, since the fall, the systems of this world, the customs, the philosophy, manners and behaviour of people are mostly quite opposite and contrary to the will of God.

Before the fall, God gave man the authority to rule the world and have dominion over it.

> *So God created man in his own image, in the image of God created he him; male and female created he them.* Genesis 1:27

With the fall, man became subject to Satan who effectively usurped the authority God had given to man over

the earth. From that time the whole world came under
the influence of the devil, the wicked one. He became
the 'god' or the 'prince' of this world (John 14:30; 16:11;
2 Corinthians 4:4) controlling men and women through
sin and diverse lusts, and blinding people to the truth
of the Gospel, turning men to be haters of God, adopting
principles quite opposed to God's Word as their lifestyle.
This is why homosexuals do not see anything wrong in
their sinful practice, calling it an alternative lifestyle.
This is why abortionists think they have a right to take
little babies' lives. This is why two unmarried people
co-habit, living in sin, and thinking they are having fun.
Having been blinded by the prince of this world, they see
wrongs as rights and blacks as whites.

*In whom the god of this world hath blinded the
minds of them who believe not, lest the light of the
glorious gospel of Christ, who is the image of God,
should shine unto them.* 2 Corinthians 4:4

John writing to believers in his time wrote the following:

*And we know that we are of God, and the whole
world lieth in wickedness.* 1 John 5:19

Other translations give us a clearer meaning of what
the Spirit is saying here.

*We know that we belong to God even though the
whole world is under the rule of the Evil One.*
Good News Bible

*We know that we are children of God, and that the
whole world is under the control of the evil one.*
NIV

The World

> *We know that we ourselves are children of God, and we also know that the world around us is under the power of the evil one.*   JB Phillips

> *We know that we are children of God and that all the rest of the world around us is under Satan's power and control.*   Living Bible

The message is very clear from these verses that the whole world is under the influence of the devil. It is only those who are truly born again that are free from this influence, and the dominion of the evil one. They belong to God. They can live, using their spiritual authority to cause the glory of God to overcome the influence of the devil. That is why we have to be victorious over the world and all its satanic influences, that the glory of God may shine forth through our lives.

World Attitude And God

The principles and philosophy of the world oppose God's principles. And for a child of God to please Him, he has to have victory over the negative attitude of the world, and live by the Word of God.

While God ordained that His people should walk and live by faith, the world's standard is to walk by sight. God says 'If you believe thou shalt see . . .'. That is to say believe first, and then you will see. The world would say 'seeing is believing'.

If a child of God is not walking in victory over the ways of this world, he will be carnal and walk by sight. It will be difficult for him to receive a miracle from God, be it healing, deliverance or provision, because, instead of believing, he will struggle to see before he believes. And until you actually believe and count the thing as done, you cannot receive anything from God. *'If thou wouldest believe, thou shouldest see the glory of God'* John 11:40. This is why the people of the world find it difficult to believe miracles. Since the miraculous transcends reason, they doubt it. Why? They cannot explain it on the platform of reason. But why must it be thought incredible to you that God should raise the dead? God is God and man is man.

With man there are too many impossibilities but with God, nothing shall be impossible. The man who will overcome this worldly attitude of unbelief will be like Smith Wigglesworth who said 'I am not moved by what I see, I am not moved by what I hear, I am not moved by what I feel. I am only moved by the word of God.' To live by faith is to overcome the world. The just shall live by faith.

God is holy. The people that worship Him or serve Him must do so with a pure heart and clean hands. The design of God is that His people be delivered from their enemy, and to serve Him in holiness and righteousness all the days of their lives.

The oath which he swore to our father, Abraham,
   That he would grant unto us that we, being delivered out of the hand of our enemies, might serve him without fear,
   In holiness and righteousness before him, all the days of our life.   Luke 1:73–75

The Lord wants our hearts to be perfect towards Him. He wants us to be holy and righteous in our motives, in our thinking and in our actions.

It is obvious that the attitude of the world is quite

contrary to this. Terrible sins and iniquities are being committed with eagerness and greed. Hatred, bitterness, envy, impurities and all things that defile, are the normal way of life of the world. And anybody who seeks to abide by God's standard makes himself a prey. At schools and colleges, chastity and purity is considered old fashioned. Immorality, unbelief are the norms. Young folks now experiment with sex. The adults cannot correct and rebuke them because they too have gone the way of the world. But God's people are called to be holy as He our God is holy.

But as he which hath called you is holy, so be ye holy in all manner of conversation.   1 Peter 1:15

Honesty and Integrity

The people of the world are hardly honest. Even those who pretend to be honest before the public, do so purely for selfish motives – either to protect their reputation or for fear of disgrace, or to promote their enterprises. It is never out of a supreme regard for the authority of God neither is it for the love of humanity. That is why they can pretend to be pious in public but privately and in 'little' matters they show the truth of their heart and their normal dishonesty.

While studying the Scriptures recently the Lord inpressed on me again that the root of genuine honesty and integrity is the fear of the Lord. When a man walks in the fear of the Lord he will live straight and honestly.

Having, therefore, these promises, dearly beloved, let us cleanse ourselves from all filthiness of the flesh and spirit, perfecting holiness in the fear of God. 2 Corinthians 7:1

Since we have these promises, dear friends, let us purify ourselves from everything that contaminates body and spirit, perfecting holiness out of reverence for God. 2 Corinthians 7:1 NIV

Wholesome fear of God. Reverence for God. That is the root of solid integrity and true holiness. No wonder all true virtue in society is crumbling. Homes are breaking up. Corruption ruins businesses and destroys governments. The moral fabric of society is disintegrating because we have thrown away the fear of the Lord and are trying to build on worldly, humanistic, secular philosophy. But a child of God is called to repudiate the ungodly philosophy of the world and embrace the fear of the Lord.

The fear of the LORD is the beginning of wisdom, and the knowledge of the Holy One is understanding.
Proverbs 9:10

Selfishness is a terrible sin. But it is the normal attitude of the men of the world. People seek nothing but their self-interest. They don't think about what they should contribute or give to make a venture succeed. Even when they do, it is usually not selfless, but in order to get a reward. Couples are selfish in marriage relationships. Business partners selfishly cheat one another. Leaders and people in important positions use their posts for selfish ends. Everybody is out for what he can get. Everybody is grabbing endlessly. And thus, selfishness separates friends, destroys homes, causes people to lose their jobs and destabilises nations.

But what is God's attitude? *'For God SO LOVED the world, that HE GAVE . . .'* John 3:16. Instead of being selfish, God is love. Instead of looking for what He can get, He gave us something we could never have or merit. He gave us eternal life through His only begotten Son. His attitude, as opposed to the world's is exemplified in His Word. *'It is more blessed to give than to receive'* Acts 20:35. Imagine everybody in the world beginning to practise these principles of love and charity instead of selfishness. What a wonderful place this earth would be.

God loves sincerity and truth. In fact, anyone who wants to walk with God must be sincere and true. But see how men take great pains to cover up the true state of their hearts. They will appear to be pious whereas they are wicked. They will want to show that they are religious and devoted whereas they are corrupt and disobedient to God. People want to have a good image. They are not ready to be sincere and open. Yet to know and walk with God, sincerity and truth are indispensable. You have to be sincere and be your real self. Remove your mask and be open to God.

Ostentation, showmanship and self-parade are the common attitudes of the people of the world. For any little good they do they make a loud noise about it that they may receive the praise of men. In dressing, worldly people can be very flamboyant and flashy simply to attract attention. Many ladies in the world have virtually thrown virtue to the wind. They know nothing about *'the ornament of a meek and quiet spirit, which is in the sight of God of great price'* 1 Peter 3:4. Their desire is never to glorify God in all they do. They clothe themselves attractively outside to cover their inward rottenness. The Bible says *'it is a shame even to speak of those things which are done of them in secret'* Ephesians 5:12. Yet they appear very gorgeous outside. This is worldliness. It is opposed to the will and the Word of God. To have victory over the world is to overcome these sinful and selfish tendencies, to stay true to God, pure and honest and to live in the world without allowing the world to defile you with these negative attitudes.

All men were one time or other under the negative influence of the world. All of us were born sinners, *'Behold, I was shaped in iniquity, and in sin did my mother conceive me'* Psalm 51:5. Hence we were all under the dominion of the evil one. We partook of the corruption, ungodliness of this world. But when you received Jesus as your Lord and Saviour, a change took place. It is very remarkable, if truly you have been saved. The authority of the devil was broken in your life and Jesus became your Lord. God delivered you from the kingdom of darkness and translated you into the Kingdom of His Son, Jesus.

> *. . . The Father [God] . . . hath delivered us from the power of darkness, and hath translated us into the kingdom of his dear Son.* Colossians 1:12–13

You received a new nature – the nature of God – and you were born again. You were delivered from the corruption and lusts that are in the world and you were made holy unto God. Speaking about children of God the Bible says:

> *According as his divine power hath given unto us all things that pertain unto life and godliness, through the knowledge of him that hath called us to glory and virtue;*
> *By which are given unto us exceedingly great*

The World

and precious promises, that by these ye might be partakers of the divine nature, having escaped the corruption that is in the world through lust.
2 Peter 1:3–4

Furthermore, the Word of God says:

And you hath he quickened, who were dead in trespasses and sins;
In which in times past ye walked according to the course of this world, according to the prince of the power of the air, the spirit that now worketh in the children of disobedience;
Among whom also we all had our conversation in times past in the lusts of our flesh, fulfilling the desires of the flesh and of the mind, and were by nature the children of wrath, even as others.
Ephesians 2:1–3

Please note the language of the Holy Spirit here and the tenses He uses in describing a born-again Christian. He was once dead in trespasses and sins, but now he has been made alive. In the past he used to walk according to the course of this world, i.e. behaving like every other person in the world but now a transformation has taken place within him. Formerly he used to walk in the flesh but now he walks in the Spirit. He was by nature the child of wrath, but now by nature he is a child of God. In summary, using the words of the apostle Peter, he has *'become a partaker of the divine nature and has escaped the corruption that is in the world through lust.'* 2 Peter 1:4. Or, using the word of the apostle Paul he has been delivered *'from this present evil world, according to the will of God and our Father'* Galatians 1:4. And that is why he can have victory over the world.

You cannot have victory over the world unless you have been born again (1 John 5:5). If these things are not true of you, you have to give your heart to Jesus now and be born again.

For whatever is born of God overcometh the world; and this is the victory that overcometh the world, even our faith.
Who is he that overcometh the world, but he that believeth that Jesus is the Son of God? 1 John 5:4–5

The believer has been saved from the world. He now belongs to Christ, even though he is still in the world, surrounded by all the practices and habits of the world. Although he is in the world, he is not of the world. Our Lord Jesus says:

They are not of the world, even as I am not of the world. John 17:16

This is the battle we all have to fight. We are in the world but definitely not of the world. The world presses us all around and always seek to squeeze us into its mould. Social pressure. Peer pressure. Government decisions and demands. Yet we must live in victory over the world.

This is the problem with many Christians. They still behave as if they are of the world. You are not of the world at all. You are in the world as salt – to preserve what is good and sweeten the bitter condition. You are in the world as light to shine brightly and show the world the way to God. You are in the world as Christ's ambassador, to represent Him worthily and speak for Him that the world may be reconciled to God.

This is why it is important for you as a child of

The World

God to possess the place where you are for God — your environment. You are to possess that place for God and change it for better. This is the plan of God. He wants us to reign like kings with Him, exercise our spiritual authority to influence the world, and bring the world to Christ.

Ye are the salt of the earth : . . .
Ye are the light of the world. A city that is set on an hill cannot be hidden . . .
Let your light so shine before men, that they may see your good works, and glorify your Father, who is in heaven.   Matthew 5:13–15

Chapter Seven

How The World Affects The Christian

Having established the fact that a born again child of God is already saved from the corruption in the world we should know that the world is constantly seeking to defile the child of God. We will examine the ways this happens.

The first way is through **anxiety and the cares of this world**. We have certain basic needs and concerns in this world as human beings: what to eat, what to wear, where to live, who to marry, how to make progress, passing exams, getting good jobs, having children and so on. Having desires, and working to have these needs met is normal and legitimate. But this can easily degenerate into what is known as 'the cares and the anxieties of this world'.

The normal thing for someone who is not yet born again is to worry and fret over these issues. He thinks he cannot have his needs met by his own efforts. He worries and fears and loses sleep. He does not trust in the Lord for the supply of his needs. He forgets the Giver and His gift. Many even give this as an excuse for not having time to attend to the things of God and the salvation of their souls. They are so possessed with the cares of this life that they have no thought of eternity. This is wrong. And this is the reason why in spite of much labour and worry much of what they desire eludes them. Some who succeed in getting what they want, do not find satisfaction and fulfilment because they do not acknowledge God, the Giver of all good things.

Victory over the world is staying free from anxiety over whatever needs and hopes may be in life. You should trust the Lord completely and believe that in His goodness and providential care, He will meet all your needs. Jesus Christ the Lord said:

Take no thought for your life, what ye shall eat; neither for the body, what ye shall put on . . .

Consider the ravens; for they neither sow nor reap, which neither have storehouse nor barn, and God feedeth them; how much more are ye better than the fowls? . . .

Consider the lilies how they grow. They toil not, they spin not; and yet I say unto you that Solomon, in all his glory, was not arrayed like one of these.

If, then, God so clothe the grass, which is today in the field, and tomorrow is cast into the oven, how much more will he clothe you, O ye of little faith?
Luke 12:22, 24, 27, 28

Jesus wants us to have confidence that the Lord, our Father, will provide all our needs according to His riches in glory. He said that God even cares enough for His creatures as to provide for the birds of the air and the lilies of the valley.

Many of us do not think that we are more valuable to God than birds and flowers. We do not seem to know that He cares more for us than for them. Why are you anxious and fretful? After all your worries cannot do a thing. It is when you trust in the Lord and exercise your faith that you get your needs met, not when you fret.

I have seen children of God worry over many things – money, what to eat and many other things. Many have so worried themselves that they are in constant distress and fear. Worrying over such issues is behaving like the people of the world. It is worldly and sinful. God does not say you should worry. He said you should *'cast all your care upon him, for he careth for you'* 1 Peter 5:7. Many do not cast their cares on the Lord and they fall under the weight of these cares.

To overcome the world is to overcome worldly anxieties. It is to trust the Lord and rest confidently in His providential care to meet your needs exactly, to see you through in life. Therefore,

Fret not thyself because of evildoers, neither be thou envious against the workers of iniquity.

For they shall soon be cut down like the grass, and wither like the green herb.

Trust in the LORD, and do good; so shalt thou dwell in the land, and verily thou shalt be fed.

Delight thyself also in the LORD, and he shall give thee the desires of thine heart.

Commit thy way unto the LORD; trust also in him, and he shall bring it to pass. Psalm 37:1–5

I do not mean for you to abandon your legitimate duty. For example, a student should work hard and prepare for his exams. A man should work hard to get a means of living, *'for he that will not work neither let him eat'*. But you should not allow anxiety and fear. Trust in the Lord and be confident in Him. And if you already have a load of cares, cast them upon the Lord. Let Him do the caring while you do the believing and receiving.

> *Be anxious for nothing, but in everything by prayer and supplication, with thanksgiving, let your requests be made known to God; and the peace of God, which surpasses all understanding, will guard your hearts and minds through Christ Jesus.* **Philippians 4:6–7 NKJV**

Pride Of Life

People want to be great. They are high-minded. They want to be anything you can imagine – a millionaire, a great scholar, a well-known preacher, a super-star for Jesus. Their reasons for this is that they may be well-known and influential, someone to reckon with in society. And they use all possible means to achieve their aim. This is the pride of life.

Becoming great is not sinful in itself. After all Jesus Christ is still and will ever be the greatest and most unique person in history. But why do you want to be what you want to be? These are days of political awareness and Christians are going into politics. These are days of industrial explosions, Christians are going into business. It is God's desire to bless His children and place them high, to make them heads and not tails.

Our desire to be great must be God-centred. If it is God-centred and for the good of humanity, the Lord will surely grant that desire. Anything other than this is pride of life. If you sincerely desire what you want to be for God and the good of humanity, then the Lord Himself will see to it that you are what you should be. But to seek great things for yourself and not that God may be glorified is pride.

I read a story told by Dr T.L. Osborn. When he was

a young preacher he met with Dr F.F. Bosworth, then an elderly minister of about 75 years of age. Dr Osborn said F.F. Bosworth took him aside for counsel and said, 'Young man, if you want what God wants, and for the same reason that God wants it, then you will always have God by your side and will be as invincible as God'. That is the key issue: wanting what God wants, for the same reason as God wants it. Otherwise, it is vanity and high-mindedness.

The world has so affected many Christians that they have become high-minded in their tastes. This shows in what they wear, their homes, how they conduct their affairs and the words they speak. There is no distinction between them and the people of the world.

God hates high-mindedness (Proverbs 16:18). It is one of the characteristics of wicked men in these last days (2 Timothy 3:4). And the Bible tells us to charge those who are rich not to be high-minded and selfish, but humble and lowly.

Charge them that are rich in this world, that they be not high-minded, nor trust in uncertain riches, but in the living God, who giveth us richly all things to enjoy;

That they do good, that they be rich in good works, ready to distribute, willing to communicate [share]. 1 Timothy 6:17–18

No proud or high-minded person can be of any use in God's hands – whether in spiritual affairs or in our day-to-day affairs and work. No high-minded person can receive any revelation from the Lord either in the Word or by the Spirit of God. It takes humility and faith to seek God. And God has no blessing for the high-minded, in fact He resists them (1 Peter 5:6). If the spirit of this

How The World Affects The Christian

world has a chance of gripping you, either in the form of love of riches, position, fame or knowledge, it will choke the Word of God out of you and cause you to become unfruitful and useless in the things of God. When Jesus was speaking on the parable of the Sower, He said that the word that fell among thorns represents those who allow the care of this world and the deceitfulness of its riches to choke the Word in their lives.

> *He also that received seed among the thorns is he that heareth the word; and the care of this world, and the deceitfulness of riches, choke the word, and he becometh unfruitful.* Matthew 13:22

> *And these are they that are sown among thorns; such as hear the word,*
> *And the cares of this world, and the deceitfulness of riches, and the lusts of other things entering in, choke the word, and it becometh unfruitful'* Mark 4:18–19

> *And that which fell among thorns are they who, when they have heard, go forth, and are choked with cares and riches and pleasures of this life.*
> Luke 8:14

You can see how the Word of God can become unfruitful in people. We have known some folks who, when they were either at the Higher School or the Polytechnic were strong in the Lord and full of the Word of God. But entering into the University they allowed the cares of this world and the pride of life to choke the Word of God in them. We have also known people who were fruitful and effective Christians when in the University, but getting out into the outside world, they allowed the pride of life and the cares of the world to choke the Word of God in them. More painfully, we have known some men of God, divinely called, anointed of the Spirit, with their ministries confirmed with signs and wonders, sink low because they allowed the pride of life to enter into their lives and ministries.

A child of God should overcome the world. And to overcome the world is to overcome high-mindedness and pride and to be all you want for God. It is to be truly humble, meek and lowly even when you enjoy great privileges which others do not enjoy – you should use these privileges to glorify God.

Paul the apostle was someone who could have been high-minded. He was a Jew (which was a thing of pride). He was a Pharisee. He was learned. He was an apostle. He had done so much for God. But he had thoroughly overcome the pride of life and was fully subdued to Christ. He said:

> *But what things were gain to me, those I counted loss for Christ.*
> *Yea doubtless, and I count all things but loss for the excellency of the knowledge of Christ Jesus my Lord; for whom I have suffered the loss of all things, and do count them but dung, that I may win Christ.* Philippians 3:7–8

This should be your attitude. Be victorious over the world as you live your life to the glory of God.

> *Whether, therefore, ye eat, or drink, or whatever ye do, do all to the glory of God.* 1 Corinthians 10:31

Compromise

This is a very dangerous but subtle way the world can affect children of God. When people know you are a

Christian, they may not bother to discourage you. But they will want you to compromise your stand, water down the quality of your Christian life, compromise your conviction and eventually be conformed to the world.

Often it is an attempt to avoid persecution and win favour that makes many Christians compromise their stand. Such Christians enter a state of apathy. Nothing moves them – either to pray seriously, fast or take some daring steps for the Lord. No zeal, no zest, just a passive state of being. And they swallow all sorts of suggestions that their unbelieving counterparts bring, even though it is a clear departure from the Word of God. This is compromise. In an attempt not to upset their co-workers they refuse to share Christ with them. Instead of taking an open and decisive stand for Christ they are 'secret disciples'. Instead of possessing the place where they are for God and making Jesus Lord of the place, they just keep quiet and allow the devil to do anything he likes. How many Christians are in this state of compromise and conformity to the world? It is time to change for the better.

If all Christians in this nation were awake and were all out for Christ, taking an open stand for Him at work, at school, at home; if all Christians were aflame for Christ, preaching Him to every sinner around them and urging them to be saved, what a great change this would bring to this nation.

Many terrible things happen in places where there are Christians. We have not learnt to properly use our spiritual authority and the weapons of our warfare.

He that overcomes the world does not compromise his stand. He does not dance to the tune of the world. He casts aside the fear of what men would say and uses all his energy to lift up the banner of Christ wherever he is. You should be an overcomer.

Friendship With The World

This is one of the greatest dangers the world poses to a child of God. But it need not be a danger if the child of God knows who he is and knows what his attitude should be to the world, and acts accordingly.

The world will want to get your attention and to court your friendship. While you are to relate meaningfully with the people of the world and bring them to Christ you are not to be in love with the world. Know that friendship with the world is enmity with God.

> *Ye adulterers and adulteresses, know ye not that the friendship of the world is enmity with God? Whosoever, therefore, will be a friend of the world is the enemy of God.* James 4:4

There have been cases when an unbeliever desperately wants to marry a child of God. They do everything to succeed. Make up your mind once and for all. There is no deep relationship that should exist between you and the world. These people of the world need you only to meet their needs, and that is not true love. And as a matter of fact, the Lord warned against the unequal yoke. No child of God is allowed to enter into any deep relationship with an unbeliever either in business or in marriage. And the people that do this are disobedient to the Word of God, and they soon find out that they are wrong.

How The World Affects The Christian

> *Be ye not unequally yoked together with unbelievers; for what fellowship hath righteousness with unrighteousness? And what communion hath light with darkness?*
>
> *And what concord hath Christ with Belial? Or what part hath he that believeth with an infidel?*
>
> *And what agreement hath the temple of God with idols? For ye are the temple of the living God; as God hath said, I will dwell in them, and walk in them; and I will be their God, and they shall be my people.*
> 2 Corinthians 6:14–16

'Fellowship . . . Communion . . . Concord . . . Part . . . Agreement . . .' What words to express intimacy, such a relationship is forbidden between a believer who is from now on referred to as 'righteousness . . . light . . . Christ . . . he that believeth . . . the temple of God', with an unbeliever who is referred to as 'unrighteousness . . . darkness . . . Belial . . . an infidel . . . idol'.

And if you are already involved in such an unequal yoke, it is not too late. It can be broken. Only allow Christ – be it in business partnership or in a promise to marry an unbeliever. The Lord says you should come out of the relationship and be separate.

> *Wherefore, come out from among them, and be ye separate, saith the Lord, and touch not the unclean thing; and I will receive you,*
>
> *And will be a Father unto you, and ye shall be my sons and daughters, saith the Lord Almighty.*
> 2 Corinthians 6:17–18

You should come out of such relationships. If you are already joined to your partner in marriage, you can only pray for his or her conversion. There is nothing you can do about the relationship. If you are not yet joined in marriage, do not be disobedient, come out and be separate unto the Lord. If you are willing and obedient, you will eat the good of the land.

Apart from this, love for the things of this world, love for riches, positions and material things is at variance with the will of God. And he who overcomes the world does not love the things of the world at all.

Love not the world, neither the things that are in the world. If any man love the world, the love of the Father is not in him.

For all that is in the world, the lust of the flesh, and the lust of the eyes, and the pride of life, is not of the Father, but is of the world.

And the world passeth away, and the lust of it; but he that doeth the will of God abideth forever.
1 John 2:15–17

Chapter Eight

Victory Over The World

The Lord wants to bring every child of His to a place of complete and continuous victory over the world. He has made adequate provision for this. It is for you to receive victory over the world by faith, and to abide in this victory.

Be Crucified To The World

You have to be crucified, and die to the world and all it holds dear. To be crucified to the world is to regard the things of the world in the light of eternity. You do not have a do-or-die attitude to the things of the world. They do not possess you. They do not master you. But you master and use them for God's glory. Paul said: *'But God forbid that I should glory, save in the cross of our Lord Jesus Christ, by whom the world is crucified unto me, and I unto the world'* Galatians 6:14. The world was crucified, stripped naked to Paul. There was nothing in the world that attracted him. Only Christ. Likewise he himself was crucified to the world. The world had nothing to desire in Paul. No wonder he told the Corinthians that he did not desire to know anything among them except Jesus, and Him crucified. He was not looking for their money, or recognition, or titles or honours. Only Jesus. That is the man that has been crucified to the world.

He later admonished them that in view of the shortness of time and the iminent coming of our Lord Jesus Christ, they should be people who use the things of this world but are not engrossed in them. That is still the right attitude every believer should have to the world. Use it but don't abuse it, don't befriend it, because the things of this world shall pass away.

Total Surrender

Secondly, yield your whole being to God and trust Him to meet all your needs.

This is important. If you are still fretting and holding on to your life firmly, as if you can keep it by yourself, you have not known victory over the world. Let go of your life. Yield it entirely to Christ. Let Him possess you. Let Him drive out the love of the world and fill you with His love from above by the Holy Spirit. Let Him direct you and meet your needs according to His providential care. He loves you and He cares for you. Remember His Word. *'For whosoever would save his life shall lose it; but whosoever will lose his life for my sake, the same shall save it'* Luke 9:24. Let Him take absolute control of your life and use it for His glory.

> *I beseech you therefore, brethren, by the mercies of God, that ye present your bodies a living sacrifice, holy, acceptable unto God, which is your reasonable service.*
>
> *And be not conformed to this world, but be ye transformed by the renewing of your mind, that ye*

may prove what is that good, and acceptable, and perfect, will of God. Romans 12:1–2

Be Heavenly Minded

To have victory over the world you must also be heavenly minded. To be earthly minded is to be possessed with the thoughts of the things of this earth for their own end. To be controlled and directed by the philosophy of this world, to be in love with the world and all its ungodly lusts. But remember what the Bible says.

If ye, then, be risen with Christ, seek those things which are above, where Christ sitteth on the right hand of God.

Set your affection on things above, not on things on the earth.

For ye are dead, and your life is hidden with Christ in God.

When Christ, who is our life, shall appear, then shall ye also appear with him in glory.

Colossians 3:1–4

The only thoughts that occupy the mind of many Christians are about how they shall eat, drink, marry, go to school, build a house and settle down to enjoy life. They hardly think of perishing souls, and the best way to make a solid contribution to the preaching and advancement of the Gospel; they hardly think about the rapture of the Church or the day they will stand before the judgment seat of Christ to receive their reward for all their labours on earth.

Start to set your thinking right. Think on things of

eternal value and be heavenly minded. There is great peace and reward herein.

Worse still, many others have allowed their minds to be filled with all the worldly rubbish that is being projected daily on the television and radio, in the newspapers and the barrage of suggestive advertisements. Hence they have become impure in their thinking and worldly in their attitude. Why don't you fill your mind with the Word of God? Why don't you switch over to the Holy Spirit and let Him fill your thought and your whole being? The Bible urges us not to let worldly and carnal issues dominate our thoughts but that we should guard our hearts with all diligence; that we should think on things that are pure and true. You can, if you will. The Holy Spirit stands ready to help you do it.

Keep thy heart with all diligence; for out of it are the issues of life.   Proverbs 4:23

Finally, brethren, whatever things are true, whatever things are honest, whatever things are just, whatever things are pure, whatever things are lovely, whatever things are of good report; if there be any virtue, and if there be any praise, think on these things.

Those things which ye have both learned, and received, and heard, and seen in me, do, and the God of peace shall be with you. Philippians 4:8–9

Walk By Faith

For whatever is born of God overcometh the world; and this is the victory that overcometh the world, even our faith.   1 John 5:4

Victory Over The World

You will have to begin to take God on His Word. What He promises, He will do. You will have to believe God. Exercise your faith to have your needs met. You must exercise your faith and keep your heart on the Lord even in the midst of troubles. He will keep you in perfect peace. You will have to walk by faith and not fall into the realm of senses and emotions again. It takes faith to please God. He wants us to walk by faith and not by sight. We will be blessed and happy if we believe Him and confidently trust that He will make His Word good. The way to overcome the world is to walk by faith. The Bible says: *'The just shall live by faith'* Galatians 3:11. This simply implies that the day the righteous man begins to walk other than by faith, he will begin to run into trouble. Live and walk by faith therefore, beloved, and your victory over the world is certain.

Chapter Nine

Abiding In Victory Over The World

It is not enough to have victory over the world, you have to abide in this victory and walk continually in it. It is not God's will that we run in and out of victory. Victorious today, defeated tomorrow. Up on the mountain today, down in the valley tomorrow. Such inconsistent Christian life is not God's will for you. God wants you to enjoy complete victory over the world all of the time. This is what the Bible says about Jesus, and the victory He has secured for us.

But thanks be to God, who giveth us the victory through our Lord Jesus Christ. 1 Corinthians 15:57

God gives us the victory through our Lord Jesus Christ. This is put in the present continuous tense. He gives us the victory . . . all the time. Not just intermittently, but always and continuously. Paul made it clearer in another scripture.

Now thanks be unto God, who always causeth us to triumph in Christ, and maketh manifest the savour of his knowledge by us in every place.
2 Corinthians 2:14

Abiding in Victory Over The World

Did you read that? God **always causes** us to triumph in Christ Jesus . . . **in every place**. Alleluia. No matter **what** the battle is, God always causes us to triumph. No matter **when** the battle comes, He always causes us to triumph. No matter **where** the battle comes from, He always causes us to triumph. This is the will of God for you – continuous victory over the world at all times, and in every place and situation.

But how can this be? It is a logical question.

First, and foremost, trust God completely for your victory. It is only God that gives us the victory. The flesh profits nothing. Victory over the world is *'not by might, nor by power, but by my Spirit, says the Lord'* Zechariah 4:6.

Apart from a definite resolution in your heart to have victory over the world, there must be a conscious dependence on the Holy Spirit. Your victory comes by God through the Holy Spirit. Hence trust Him for it.

Secondly, take time to renew your mind constantly with the Word of God. The surest way you can escape being conformed again to the world is to be transformed by the renewing of your mind.

And be not conformed to this world, but be ye transformed by the renewing of your mind. Romans 12:2

Your mind is renewed by constantly meditating on the Word of God and by praying. Take time to study the Word of God and you find that you are being transformed into the image of Christ. This is very necessary if you want to abide in victory over the world. Many believers do not take time to study the Word. They read the Scriptures carnally and depend on what they hear preached on Sundays alone. This is not good enough. We are to meditate in the Word of God day and night. When you do, the Word of God will cleanse you continuously from the corrupting influence of the world and strengthen you to withstand all its pressure. If you are not loaded with God's Word and power you will collapse under the pressure of the world around you, you will not be able to stand up to it. Therefore, beloved, fill yourself with God's Word. When you do, you arm yourself for complete victory over the world.

Thirdly, take time to fellowship with God's people regularly. When you meet with the people of God and share fellowship with them you are challenged, quickened and revived. As you share your testimonies and the Word of God together, you see clearly the need to be separated from the world and worthily represent Christ on earth. Fellowship with children of God considerably reduces the possibility of entering into fellowship with the world. As you meet with the people of God, you sharpen and strengthen one another.

Iron sharpeneth iron; so a man sharpeneth the countenance of his friend. Proverbs 27:17

This is why the Bible admonishes us not to give up meeting with God's people. Some claim to be believers but are negligent and lackadaisical when it comes to going to services or for fellowship. To such people these scriptures are written out.

Let us not give up meeting together, as some are in the habit of doing, but let us encourage one another – and all the more as you see the Day approaching. Hebrews 10:25 NIV

I was glad when they said unto me, Let us go into the house of the LORD. Psalm 122:1

Make up your mind to become regular in services and fellowships. Go with all the members of your family. That is where you truly belong. The time of service is not the time to attend club meetings, a family meeting, or a sporting or recreational event. There is time for everything. The time for services and fellowship with other children of God should be strictly observed and you will profit greatly by it.

Yet there are believers who are truly born again but do not have a church they call their own. They are not under any pastoral care. They roam from one church to another. This is not biblical. God does not want any of His children to be a sheep without a shepherd. He wants us to come under the pastoral care of a godly man, who has been called and anointed to shepherd God's flock. These days, God has raised and is raising many of such genuine shepherds. Find such a one and identify fully with him, and be fed regularly from God's Word. Your life will become better.

Commitment

A solid commitment to world evangelism is another way of walking in victory over the world. We should all be diligently committed to getting the Gospel message to all the world before Jesus' return.

Some children of God are not committed to a serious Gospel venture – either in their church, school or locality. They are not involved in partnership with any Christian ministry that is truly gathering the end-time harvest. Because of this they have no vision of the world's need and consequently are idle. Being idle, they could not possibly have victory; the devil easily finds work for them. The adversary finds for them alternatives that waste their resources and time. What they refuse to spend for the Lord the enemy steals by force. This should not happen to you.

Have a vision for the world's need. Make efforts to win souls. Team up with other children of God around you – in your church, at school, around your home, and see how you can show the world that Jesus changes life. Get involved with a serious God-anointed ministry that is winning the lost and blessing the Body of Christ. We have a message for the world. The message is unique. It is the only message that can transform the hearts of men and restore the original image of God in them. This message must be got across to the world and you have a part to play in it.

The communists do not have a message at all. Neither do the socialists. Their theories have not been able to give peace to the earth. Neither can it give a hope beyond the grave. Yet they could die for their empty theories and vain propaganda. Shouldn't we arise and proclaim boldly this Good News of Jesus Christ our Lord? Shouldn't we publish this message of salvation? You have a part to play. Do not be idle any longer. Be committed somewhere and give the best of your time, talent, money and heart to the propagation of the only message that is capable of making wicked men righteous, giving them the hope of heaven.

Who Is He That Overcomes?

God has made provision for the child of God to overcome the world. It is only a matter of knowing who you are in Christ, what God has done for you in Christ and assuming your position of authority over the world. We are to reign like kings with Christ over the world and

Abiding in Victory Over The World

over the devil. This is the portion of everyone who has accepted Jesus as his Lord and Saviour.

> *For if by one man's offence [Adam] death reigned by one, much more they who receive abundance of grace and of the gift of righteousness shall reign in life by one, Jesus Christ.* Romans 5:17

But there is nobody that can have victory over the world except those who have received Jesus Christ as their Lord and Saviour. If you have not, you can do so now. Then you can have victory over the world.

> *For whatever is born of God overcometh the world; and this is the victory that overcometh the world, even our faith.*
> *Who is he that overcometh the world, but he that believeth that Jesus is the Son of God?* 1 John 5:4–5

Chapter Ten

Your Adversary

Satan is very much around in the world today — stirring people to sin, rebelliousness and disobedience to God; putting people in bondage and fear; tormenting people with sicknesses, diseases and different afflictions.

Many do not believe the devil exists at all. They think the subject 'Satan' is just an idea, a figment of the human imagination. The devil torments them daily in different forms but keeps them ignorant of it.

In Job the Lord asked the devil about his movements and where he had just come from. He answered: *'From going to and fro in the earth, and from walking up and down in it'* Job 1:7.

Doing what?

Stealing, killing and destroying.

> *The thief cometh not but to steal, and to kill, and to destroy; I am come that they might have life, and that they might have it more abundantly.*
>
> John 10:10

The devil, or Satan, is the thief referred to here by Jesus Christ. He is very much around. The individual who has not been born again is under his influence and control. The Bible refers to such people as being in the kingdom

Your Adversary

of darkness, or under the powers of darkness, or under the influence of the spirit of disobedience, and blinded by the devil to the glorious light of the Gospel of Christ.

> *And you He made alive, who were dead in trespasses and sins, in which you once walked according to the course of this world, according to the prince of the power of the air, **the spirit who now works in the sons of disobedience**, among whom also we all once conducted ourselves in the lusts of our flesh, fulfilling the desires of the flesh and of the mind, and were by nature children of wrath, just as the others.*
> Ephesians 2:1–3 NKJV (emphasis mine)

> *Who hath delivered us from the power of darkness, and hath translated us into the kingdom of his dear Son.* Colossians 1:13

The Bible is very clear. Those who are not yet born again are the 'children of disobedience'. The spirit that is at work in them is the devil.

> *But if our gospel be hidden, it is hidden to them that are lost,*
> *In whom the god of this world hath blinded the minds of them who believe not, lest the light of the glorious gospel of Christ, who is the image of God, should shine unto them.* 2 Corinthians 4:3–4

The devil is referred to here as '*the god of this world*'. His principal job is to blind the minds of people to the glorious light of the Gospel and prevent them from being born again.

If you are born again, the Bible says you have been delivered from the power of darkness, and translated into the Kingdom of Jesus – the Kingdom of light. This means that the moment you are born again, the dominion of Satan ends in your life once and for all.

Although every born-again believer is free from his dominion, yet Satan seeks to oppress their minds, buffet their bodies, steal the blessings God has given them and, if possible, bring them into bondage again.

The devil is your personal enemy, he is no friend. He hates you and you should know it. He has a plan for you whether you are born again or not. His plan is clearly stated:

> *The thief cometh not but to steal, and to kill, and to destroy . . .* John 10:10

He wants to rob you of all that God has provided for you – salvation, good health, financial blessings, successes, prosperity, your home, your joy, your peace and your hope of eternal salvation. He wants to hinder you from realising God's purpose for your life. He wants to separate you from God and destroy you and yours. He did this to Job, before God restored all things back to him. The devil stole Job's oxen, killed his servants, destroyed his children, and then struck him with sicknesses (Job 1). But Job believed God. He did not forsake the Lord because of this wickedness of the devil. The Lord eventually gave him victory over the enemy and restored to him twice as much as the devil had stolen. Blessed be the name of the Lord.

> *And the LORD turned the captivity of Job, when he prayed for his friends; also the LORD gave Job twice as much as he had before.*

Your Adversary

> *So the LORD blessed the latter end of Job more than his beginning; for he had fourteen thousand sheep, and six thousand camels, and a thousand yoke of oxen, and a thousand she asses.*
> *He had also seven sons and three daughters.*
> Job 42:10, 12–13

Many times we attribute to God what the devil is doing. This was exactly the mistake of Job which many believers still repeat today. Because Job did not know what was going on in the spiritual realm, behind the scenes, he thought God was responsible for all his woes. He said at the beginning of his troubles: *'The LORD gave, and the LORD hath taken away; blessed be the name of the LORD'* Job 1:21.

Without any doubt there are occasions when this phrase is applicable – like in the home going of an elderly Christian. But when you are robbed, deprived, hurt, and tormented, that is not God at work, that is Satan.

Do not say God caused you to fail, to suffer, to be sick, to lose a relation, miss a blessing, or be tormented. God is altogether good and every good and perfect gift comes from Him.

> *This, then, is the message which we have heard of him, and declare unto you, that God is light, and in him is no darkness at all.* 1 John 1:5

> *Every good gift and every perfect gift is from above, and cometh down from the Father of lights, with whom is no variableness, neither shadow of turning.* James 1:17

The devil is altogether evil and he is the cause of any evil thing that ever happened. When you are able to identify who is the cause of a problem, you will be able to deal with it effectively. Stop attributing to God what the devil does. God is good.

When at last the eyes of Job were opened to see that it was Satan behind his woes and calamities and that he had accused God falsely, he quickly repented. He said, '... *Behold, I am vile; what shall I answer thee? I will lay mine hand upon my mouth*' Job 40:3–5.

The Lord then moved to bless Job and to restore what the enemy had stolen in his life. He experienced complete restoration.

These last days, the devil is fighting very desperately. This is because he knows that he has very little time left before his final judgment comes. He has demons and evil spirits with which he fights. These demons are set up in their hierarchy. These are the spirits that Christians fight every day. They are many and are all around us, and are very organised. But greater is He that is in us than he that is in the world. And don't forget, Satan only took a third of the angels in heaven during his rebellion against God (Revelation 12:4). Therefore, for every demon that is against you, there are at least two good angels fighting on your side. It is these demons and fallen angels we are to contend with in spiritual warfare every day. The Bible says:

> *For we wrestle not against flesh and blood, but against principalities, against powers, against the rulers of the darkness of this world, against spiritual wickedness in high places.* Ephesians 6:12

Note the hierarchy of these demons:

- Principalities
- Powers
- Rulers of the darkness of this world
- Spiritual wickedness in high places

Your Adversary

These are the demons that control world and national politics and economy, working against God and His Kingdom, endeavouring to frustrate God's plan and the preaching of the Gospel. They control territories and are the principal movers behind wars and bloodshed.

The job of some of these demons is to try to prevent and hinder answers to the prayers of God's saints. They try to hinder holy angels and fight them. They exercise negative influences over leaders of nations of the world. They are assigned by the devil to supervise nations, cause national calamities, ungodliness and chaos, immoralities and spiritual darkness.

Remember what happened to the prophet Daniel. He was praying for the restoration of the nation of Israel. The first day he began to pray the Lord heard and sent the answer through an angel. But one of these high-ranking demons, called 'The Prince of Persia' hindered the angel for twenty-one days. Eventually the angel Michael came to help and they prevailed over this wicked spirit.

> *Then said he unto me, Fear not, Daniel; for from the first day that thou didst set thine heart to understand, and to chasten thyself before thy God, thy words were heard, and I am come for thy words.*
>
> *But the prince of the kingdom of Persia withstood me one and twenty days; but, lo, Michael, one of the chief princes, came to help me; and I remained there with the kings of Persia.*
>
> Daniel 10:12–13

In praying about national issues, we are dealing with demons. We should command that their plans be spoiled, that their counsels be made of no effect, that their wickedness and devices come to nothing. If we do not get answers immediately, we should still hold on to our confession of faith and not give up, believing God until the answers are manifested in our leaders and national issues.

Another category of demons is principally concerned with the preaching of the Gospel. They want to hinder it by any means. These are the demons that rule the hearts of the unbelieving ones and blind their eyes to the things of the Gospel. They are responsible for every work of darkness – witchcraft, juju, talisman, secret cults and societies, metaphysical movements, heresies and doctrines of demons and all things that are contrary to the truth of the Gospel. They oppose the propagation of the Word of God and hinder ministers of the Gospel. They can possess human vessels. We have to contend with and prevail over them in the name of the Lord Jesus.

Generally, Satan and his demons are behind all sin committed in the world. Just as the devil lured Adam and Eve in the garden of Eden to sin against God, these demons still do the same today. They are responsible in most cases for bondage to lust, bad habits and covetousness. They cause accidents, premature death, quarrels and divorce. They generally work wickedness, contrary to the will of God, and can use human beings as agents to carry out their wickedness.

The devil through his agents works in the life of unconverted men and women in two major ways. First, he keeps them from having a clear understanding of the Gospel or of accepting Christ Jesus as their Lord and Saviour. He can use various means to achieve this. He either makes them hate hearing the Gospel or he even removes them from where they can hear it, for he knows that *'faith cometh by hearing, and hearing by the word of God'* Romans 10:17.

He may allow them to hear but not understand the Word of God. They are confused, they do not see the need to repent and be born again. They may even understand and be convicted but are hindered from taking a decision for Christ. They postpone the time of their salvation until it is too late.

If you fall into this category, that is, you have not understood the Gospel or what it means to be born again or that you always find an excuse for not accepting Jesus as your Lord and Saviour, it is because you are allowing the devil to work in you, leading you to destruction. Hear what the Bible says:

> *But if our gospel be hidden, it is hidden to them that are lost,*
> *In whom the god of this world hath blinded the minds of them who believe not, lest the light of the glorious gospel of Christ, who is the image of God, should shine unto them.*   2 Corinthians 4:3–4

Secondly, the devil works all manner of wickedness and sin and disobedience in and through the unbelieving ones. He blinds them in sin. He afflicts their souls with trouble. Demons can even possess the unbelievers and live in their bodies. All is an attempt to make them children of wrath and take them to the lake of fire for ever.

We have seen people so bound to a habit that they cannot be freed from it – smoking, drunkenness, fornication, bad habits. Many confess that they have tried but cannot stop it. But Jesus can make you free. Just trust Him to do it now.

> *If the Son, therefore, shall make you free, ye shall be free indeed.*   John 8:36

Chapter Eleven
The Devil Is Judged

If you are a child of God, truly born again and washed in the precious blood of Jesus Christ; then you are no longer under the dominion of the devil.

Jesus Christ came and judged the devil for you and me. At first the devil met Him in the wilderness, tempted Him just as he tempted Adam, but Jesus overcame him at all points. Satan could not have authority over Him. Rather, Jesus under the anointing of the Holy Spirit went about doing good, healing all that were oppressed of the devil. *'How God anointed Jesus of Nazareth with the Holy Ghost, and with power; who went about doing good, and healing all that were oppressed of the devil; for God was with him'* Acts 10:38. He actually showed that He came into the world to destroy the works of the devil.

When it was time for the devil himself to be paralysed, Jesus said: *'Now is the judgment of this world; now shall the prince of this world [the devil] be cast [thrown] out; And I, if I be lifted up from the earth, will draw all men unto me'* John 12:31-32.

Jesus announced that He was ready to cast out the devil. The devil did not understand what this meant so he incited the people to kill Jesus. He did not know that in the wisdom of God it was in dying that Jesus would destroy the devil. Hence moving the

The Devil Is Judged

mob to kill Jesus he destroyed himself. About Jesus it is written:

> *Forasmuch, then, as the children are partakers of flesh and blood, he also himself likewise took part of the same, that through death he might destroy him that had the power of death, that is the devil,*
> *And deliver them who, through fear of death, were all their lifetime subject to bondage.*
> Hebrews 2:14–15

Before Jesus Christ died the devil did have the power of death. But Jesus met him in a combat, paralysed him and his hosts and took back the authority he had stolen from man. It was a wonderful victory.

> *And, having spoiled principalities and powers, he made a show of them openly, triumphing over them in it.*
> Colossians 2:15

Therefore the devil is a defeated foe, paralysed and spoilt. Jesus Christ did it. Hence anyone who believes Him is delivered from the kingdom and dominion of darkness, and is free indeed. The Bible asks us to give thanks to the Father '*who hath delivered us from the power of darkness, and hath translated us into the kingdom of his dear Son*' Colossians 1:13.

If you have received Jesus as your Lord and Saviour, you HAVE BEEN delivered from the power of darkness. The power of darkness is the power of the devil. You are no longer under the devil's power and authority, you are under the authority of Christ, in the Kingdom of Jesus the Son of God. Sin is of the devil. Sickness is of the devil. Bad habits are of the devil. Poverty is of the devil. Sorrow is of the devil. Since you are no longer in the kingdom of the devil he has no right to put any of these or any other negative thing on you. You have been redeemed by God. You belong to God. *'Sin shall not have dominion over you; for ye are not under the law but under grace'* Romans 6:14.

War Against The Saints

We were once slaves under the devil. But God liberated us, not only that we may be free from his power, but also that we may exercise our new authority over him who once held us in bondage. Hence the devil fights a child of God desperately.

His first weapon is ignorance. He knows that if we know fully that his dominion over us is ended, and that we now have every authority to deal with him and his demons; to command and give them orders in the name of the Lord, he has lost. Hence he fights desperately to keep the child of God from knowing fully what God has done for him. He will want to keep him away from the Word of God. If he does not succeed in that, he will seek to hinder him from understanding it. If he fails in that, he will prevent him from acting on the Word of God.

Any Christian who will study, understand and always act on the Word of God shall always be victorious over the devil. Therefore understand who you are in Christ – a child of God who is accepted in the Beloved, the righteousness of God in Christ Jesus, an heir of God and joint heir with Christ, born again, a partaker of the divine nature. Understand your exalted position in Christ, that you are seated with Him in the heavenly

The Devil Is Judged

places, over and above all demons. Understand the authority He has given you over all the powers of the devil. Understand these things from the Word of God and live accordingly.

> *Now we have received, not the spirit of the world, but the Spirit who is of God; that we might know the things that are freely given to us of God.*
> 1 Corinthians 2:12

The second weapon the devil uses against the child of God is pressure, difficulties or conflict. It may be in the form of deprivation, disappointment, distress, persecutions, or discouragement. It may be a series of calamities like accidents, theft, losses or problems in the home. He can come in many ways in order to weaken the Christian and cause him to fall, or render him useless in the service of God.

We should know that experiences like these are common to all the saints of God all over the world. We should stand firm and resist the devil steadfastly, trusting the Lord for victory. For

> *There hath no temptation taken you but such as is common to man; but God is faithful, who will not suffer you to be tempted above that ye are able, but will, with the temptation, also make a way to escape, that ye may be able to bear it.* 1 Corinthians 10:13

Let us be strong and overcome, and not crack under pressure.

Thirdly, the devil uses sin, or temptation against the children of God. This is where great care is really needed. If he cannot stop us from knowing what God has provided for us, if he cannot prevail over us through pressure and difficulties, he tries his subtle devices of sin. He knows that when we go into sin we break our fellowship with God and open the door for the devil. He knows that God Himself is displeased with us when we are defiled with sin. That was how he got Adam and Eve, David the king, Samson the anointed and a host of others.

There is something remarkable about the children of Israel in the wilderness. The king of Moab knew that by going to war with them he could not win. He tried to hire Balaam the prophet to curse them but instead of being cursed they were blessed. So then he set his women to lure them to fornication, and they fell into it. A plague broke out in the camp and several thousand of them died on the spot.

This happens to many people of God today. They have been persecuted, tried, beaten and maltreated because of Christ yet they did not fail. They experienced great hardship and went a long way with God. But when it came to temptation to sin, lust, fornication, impurities and defilement they fell flat on their faces. We should not be ignorant of the devices of the devil any longer. We should hate sin and flee from it, living a holy life for God. Jesus said we should so much abhor sin that we would rather our right eye was plucked out than it would be used in sinning.

Sin is mostly committed through the members of our body. We should yield these members to God entirely, and when the devil tempts, learn to say firmly 'No!'.

Neither yield ye your members as instruments of unrighteousness unto sin, but yield yourselves unto God, as those that are alive from the dead, and your members as instruments of righteousness unto God. Romans 6:13

The Devil Is Judged

If a Christian will overcome the devil in this area of sin and fully yield himself to God, he will be a mighty weapon in the hands of God against the devil.

There are people who have much knowledge of what God has provided for us, who can go any length for God but are not very useful and effective because they have not overcome the devil in the area of sin. But hear what is written of the Lord Jesus: *'Thou has loved righteousness, and hated iniquity; therefore, God, even thy God, hath anointed thee with the oil of gladness above thy fellows'* Hebrews 1:9. He was anointed more than any other person because he loved righteousness, and hated iniquity.

Who is the man that will purge himself from all that is filthy? Who is the man that will set his heart to love righteousness and hate iniquity? Who is the man that will determine, through the grace of God, to overcome the devil anytime he comes around with sin? He shall be a vessel of honour, a powerful weapon in the hands of the Lord.

> *Who, concerning the truth, have erred, saying that the resurrection is past already; and overthrow the faith of some.*
>
> *Nevertheless, the foundation of God standeth sure, having this seal, The Lord knoweth them that are his; and, Let every one that nameth the name of Christ depart from iniquity.*
>
> *But in a great house there are not only vessels of gold and of silver, but also of wood and of earth; and some to honour, and some to dishonour.*
>
> *If a man, therefore, purge himself from these, he shall be a vessel unto honour, sanctified, and meet [fit] for the master's use, and prepared unto every good work.* 2 Timothy 2:18–21

For the eyes of the LORD run to and fro throughout the whole earth, to show himself strong in the behalf of them whose heart is perfect toward him. Herein thou hast done foolishly; therefore, from henceforth thou shalt have wars.

2 Chronicles 16:9

The fourth weapon is wrong doctrines. Wrong doctrines are doctrines of demons. The Bible says that the devil will use this weapon against many in these last days.

Now the Spirit speaketh expressly that, in the latter times, some shall depart from the faith, giving heed to seducing spirits, and doctrines of devils,

Speaking lies in hypocrisy, having their conscience seared with a hot iron,

Forbidding to marry, and commanding to abstain from meats, which God hath created to be received with thanksgiving by them who believe and know the truth. 1 Timothy 4:1–3

Some of these doctrines are glaringly wrong, and every Spirit-filled believer knows this – such as denying the Trinity, the Virgin Birth, the Deity of Jesus, the physical resurrection of Jesus, His physical return, the reality of heaven, the eternity of hell and other fundamental issues. There should be no compromise on any of these issues and every true believer knows this. But some of these damnable heresies do not appear to be fundamental at first. They are so carefully buried in scriptures that have been distorted and misquoted that it takes the Holy Spirit to discern them. Be watchful. Teachings that give you liberty to toy with sin, or teachings that put you into legalistic bondage are not of the Lord. Teachings that make you sad instead of joyful, or teachings that confuse you instead of having a liberating and refreshing effect on your spirit may be devil-inspired. We have seen many people swallow errors and become spiritually poisoned. We have seen men anointed of the Holy Spirit swallow strange doctrines that destroyed them.

We have seen movements which started powerfully by the Holy Spirit go into bondage and confusion, either because they that began in the Spirit sought to be perfect in the flesh or that they allowed 'a little' doctrine of devils. '*A little leaven leaveneth the whole lump*' the Bible says in 1 Corinthians 5:6.

Let us steer clear of every form of error and walk in the truth. Do not be gullible. Test every spirit, prove all things and hold fast to the truth. Begin to be open and sincere in your walk with the Lord, for many of these wrong doctrines emanated from insincerity and hypocrisy. Walk in the Spirit, listen to the Holy Spirit, be led by the Holy Spirit. The Holy Spirit will lead us into all truth, never into error.

The devil also uses lack of love to fight children of God. He has used this to scatter assemblies and fellowships. He has used it to break up movements. '*He that hateth his brother is in darkness*' 1 John 2:11. Hatred is of the devil. Do not allow the seed of the devil to grow in you. Learn to love, for love is God.

> *A new commandment I give unto you, that ye love one another; as I have loved you, that ye also love one another.*

By this shall all men know that ye are my disciples, if ye have love one to another.

John 13:34–35

Don't Allow Him

The devil always seeks to oppress the child of God – bringing sickness, causing him or her to be barren, disturbing him in his mind, troubling him in his sleep, wanting to put fear and anxiety in his mind and a host of other problems.

Know this – the devil has no right to lay any of these things on you. Do you still belong to him? Do you still owe him anything? Have you not been bought with a price? Is Jesus Christ not your Lord? Has Jesus not put the devil under your feet? Why don't you use the Word of God and prayer and whip the devil? There is no room for self-pity. You are a master, the devil is the slave. Command him to take off from you all those things he seeks to lay on you, and be gone. Use your authority. Praise God. It works!

But many times we open the door for the devil to come in. God has made a hedge around you (Job 1:10) with the blood of Jesus. The devil cannot cross that boundary to oppress you unless you open the door – either through sin or disobedience.

There are some who were actively involved in the occult and demonic activities in the past, who although they have accepted Jesus Christ as their Lord yet have not confessed with their mouth by faith that they are breaking off with the devil and renouncing all past occult activities. The devil oppresses such because they still bear his marks on their bodies. Confess those wicked occult activities. Tell the devil

The Devil Is Judged

you have renounced him and that Jesus is now your Lord. Claim your deliverance and be free. And if you have the devil's materials with you destroy them all no matter how costly. The devil has no right to torment you. No! Never again. Jesus Christ is your Lord and Master.

Chapter Twelve

Why God Still Allows Satan

Some may be quick to ask: If God made Lucifer perfect and then he fell and became the devil why does God allow him to go on, causing all the problems? After all God is omnipotent and can do whatever He wants. God ought to have removed Satan from the scene.

It is a legitimate question, but God is not only all-powerful, He is all-wise. He is a God of purpose. Behind everything He does or permits, is a good reason. I believe the following are some of the reasons why God still allows the devil to be around today, long after his fall.

Character Development

First, to develop character and faith in believers.

God allows the devil to try and test our faith that we may develop spiritual strength and character and be conformed to the image of Christ.

While it is true that God's primary means of building the believers is His Word, He also takes over the devices of the devil and uses them to build us. The devil brings them to break us, but God uses them to make and build us up.

Why God Still Allows Satan

Many of the very exciting stories in the Bible would not be there if God did not allow the devil to tempt believers. Can you imagine a Bible without the story of Joseph and Potiphar's wife, or the story of Meshach, Shadrach and Abednego or the story of Daniel in the den of lions, or the classic story of Job. By the time you have taken all such classic narration of the challenge of faith out of both the Old and the New Testaments, you would have ended up with a very dull book that cannot inspire faith nor withstand the pressures and realities of life.

God did not make us robots. He made us free moral agents and he wants each of us to willingly choose to love and serve Him, though we may have what look like more comfortable alternatives. This was the case with Moses. He had the option to become Pharaoh, the king of Egypt. But by faith, he *'refused to be called the son of Pharaoh's daughter, Choosing rather to suffer affliction with the people of God, than to enjoy the pleasures of sin for a season, Esteeming the reproach of Christ greater riches than the treasures in Egypt'* Hebrews 11:24-26. That is character.

When Daniel got to Babylon, he had the opportunity to behave like the Babylonians and no one would question him. His daily portion of food was to be the king's delicacies and sumptous food that would have just been dedicated to idols. 'What does that matter?' someone else could have said. 'After all I am not bowing down to idols. God also knows that I must eat this food otherwise there will be trouble.' Not Daniel. He chose a much simpler alternative. He would have nothing to do in the remotest sense with idolatry. He determined he must flee the appearances of evil in order to please the Lord. He therefore purposed in his heart that he would not defile himself with the portion of the king's meat, nor with the wine which he drank. As far as Daniel was concerned, there must be no compromise with evil in any shade or form. He was a man of solid conviction. That is the stuff God's overcomers are made of.

There is absolutely nothing wrong with temptations. They are part of our Christian experience. The devil is only doing his job when he tempts you. Temptations only bring out those hidden things on the inside which needs to be dealt with by God so that we may live victorious lives. *'Every man is tempted, when he is drawn away of his own lust, and enticed'* James 1:14. To be tempted is not sin. Giving in to temptation is the sin. God is faithful. He does not leave us alone in the time of temptation. He sees to it that the temptation is nothing beyond our ability to withstand, and He provides ways of escape so that we can overcome the evil devices of the devil. Temptations therefore, even though devised by the devil, are used by God to develop and prove the quality of our character.

> *There hath no temptation taken you but such as is common to man; but God is faithful, who will not suffer you to be tempted above that ye are able, but will, with the temptation, also make a way to escape, that ye may be able to bear it.*
>
> 1 Corinthians 10:13

The devil will want to prove to God that we serve Him not because we love Him but because of what we receive from Him. That was the accusation Satan brought against Job. Can you imagine your children loving you only because you give them gifts from time to time. You would hate that idea. Of course you make it a point of duty to give good gifts to your children from

Why God Still Allows Satan

time to time. But you want them to love and appreciate you for who you are whether you give them gifts or not. Our heavenly Father is the same. He wants us to love and appreciate Him in spite of His gifts and blessings upon our lives. When this is so we love and hold on to Him, even when it seems His blessings are just not there.

That was exactly the point the Lord wanted to prove to Satan when He allowed him to tempt Job. Job lost virtually everything he had. The devil took all his wealth, killed his servants, and his children, and made Job desolate all in one day. Then Satan stole his health, and then turned his wife against him. He then moved his best friends to accuse him falsely, alleging that the calamities came upon him because of his sins. Job then had enough reason to rebel against God and abandon his faith. If he had done that Satan would have made his point: Job was serving God only because of the blessings. The Bible says *'If thou faint in the day of adversity, thy strength is small'* Proverbs 24:10.

Job did not falter in time of trouble. Rather he held on to God and his faith in Him. The Bible says that in all that happened *'Job sinned not, nor charged God foolishly'* Job 1:22. Rather he made bold declarations that have helped millions down the ages. Here is one:

For I know that my redeemer liveth, and that he shall stand at the latter day upon the earth;
And though after my skin worms destroy this body, yet in my flesh shall I see God;
Whom I shall see for myself, and mine eyes shall behold, and not another; though my reins [heart] be consumed within me. Job 19:25–27

That is character. The furnace of affliction only brought out the beauty of his character and devotion to God. Commenting on Job's experience in the New Testament, James said: *'Behold, we count them happy who endure. Ye have heard of the patience of Job, and have seen the end of the Lord, that the Lord is very pitiful and of tender mercy'* James 5:11.

In the final analysis, the devil in his deviousness only serves God's purpose of developing character in the saints.

To Produce Humility

Secondly, the Lord allows the devil around in order to keep the believers humble and recognise their total dependence on the Lord.

Man in comfort without any conflict tends to assume that he is invincible. We need to know that without Jesus' help and ability we can do nothing. The devil's antagonism and warfare against the saints reminds us of this again and again.

Take the case of Peter. When Jesus told the disciples that they were all going to forsake him, he was so sure it could never happen to him. Even he was going to lay down his life, he thought, there was no way he could forsake the Lord. He was so sure that he could stand.

Then the devil struck, sifting all of them like wheat. Not only did Peter flee, together with the other disciples, he vehemently denied the Lord with a curse, three times. As the Lord looked back upon Peter after the third denial, he came to himself. He had failed the Lord though he had not wanted to. But because he trusted in himself, he failed woefully. That really broke him. The truth sank in.

> *I am the vine, ye are the branches. He that abideth in me, and I in him, the same bringeth forth much fruit; for without me ye can do nothing.* John 15:5

By the time the Lord asked Peter again after His glorious resurrection whether or not Peter loved him, his answer was totally different. Truly broken, he expressed his absolute dependence upon the Lord. '*Lord, thou knowest all things; thou knowest that I love thee* (John 21:17).'

God gave Paul an abundance of revelations and gifts. The power of the Lord was so much upon his life that if he were left alone, the enemy would sow the seed of pride and cause him to fall. Hence, God permitted the devil to confront him in warfare in order to keep him humble. Paul had this thorn in his flesh, '*messenger of Satan to buffet [him] lest [he] should be exalted above measure*' 2 Corinthians 12:7.

He asked the Lord to remove this '*thorn in the flesh*' but the Lord said No. He has permitted it for a purpose. Instead he made His grace superabundantly available for Paul so that even at the face of hell's opposition, God's grace was sufficient for him. This is one of the ways Satan serves God's purpose of keeping the saints humble.

Opportunity For Warfare

Thirdly, the presence of Satan in this world provides opportunity for conflicts so that the saints may overcome and receive rewards.

No cross no crown. No crisis no victory. But when a man endures and overcomes, he shall receive a crown of glory that does not fade away. James said it. *'Blessed is the man that endureth temptation; for when he is tried, he shall receive the crown of life, which the Lord hath promised to them that love him'* James 1:12.

Peter also said it:

In this ye greatly rejoice, though now for a season, if need be, ye are in heaviness through manifold temptations;

That the trial of your faith being much more precious than of gold that perisheth, though it be tried with fire, might be found unto praise and honour and glory at the appearing of Jesus Christ. 1 Peter 1:6–7

Paul the apostle declared triumphantly at the end of his life:

I have fought a good fight, I have finished my course, I have kept the faith;

Henceforth there is laid up for me a crown of righteousness, which the Lord, the righteous judge, shall give me at that day; and not to me only, but unto all them also that love his appearing.
2 Timothy 4:7–8

Do not be discouraged therefore beloved. If we suffer with Him, it is certain we shall reign with Him.

If we suffer, we shall also reign with him; if we deny him, he also will deny us. 2 Timothy 2:12

To Demonstrate God's Grace And Power

Fourthly, Satan is allowed in the world in order to demonstrate God's grace and power.

Light shines the brightest when the darkness is thickest. Where sin abounds, grace abounds much more. If Satan is not there to work in people like Pharaoh, how do we see the glory of God's power and the victory and the miracle of the parting of the Red Sea? If the devil is not there to possess and afflict the man of Gadarene, how do we see the power of God in action to deliver and set free?

The marvels of God's grace come to light in the life of the woman, caught in the act of adultery who was brought to Jesus. Let Satan be at his worst, we know this about God, that through the greatness of His power the enemy shall submit themselves to Him (Psalm 66:3).

To Bring People To Repentance

Fifthly, Satan can also be used by God to afflict people in order to bring them to repentance that their souls may be saved in the day of Christ Jesus.

This came out clearly in the instructions of Paul the apostle to the Corinthian brethren. A man among them had committed adultery with his father's wife but he was neither sober nor penitent about it. The apostle fumed with anger against such level of unrighteousness and sins. *'Deliver such an one unto Satan for the destruction of the flesh, that the spirit may be saved in the day of the Lord Jesus . . . Therefore, put away from among yourselves that wicked person'* 1 Corinthians 5:5, 13.

Some of us today may think that is an extreme stand. No! Sin spreads like cancer. '*A little leaven leaveneth the whole lump*' 1 Corinthians 5:6. If the issue was not promptly dealt with, the whole body was in the danger of corruption. Hence they were to hand over the person to Satan to afflict him in order to bring him back to repentance. And you can be sure the devil would do a good job. After suffering in the hands of Satan, the individual came to repentance and was eventually restored into the fellowship of the church. The restoration was at the right time so that the devil could not take advantage and destroy that individual.

> *Sufficient to such a man is this punishment, which was inflicted of many.*
>
> *So that [on the contrary] ye ought rather to forgive him, and comfort him, lest perhaps such a one should be swallowed up with overmuch sorrow . . .*
>
> *Lest Satan should get an advantage of us; for we are not ignorant of his devices.*
>
> 2 Corinthians 2:6–7, 11

An Instrument For Purification

Lastly, the devil provides a furnace where the believer's life is purged of all possibilities of falling from grace.

God uses him to bring out in us all that needs His second touch. As soon as these things surface he applies the scissors of His Word to prune and purge us so we can be pure and holy and fit for heaven.

Why God Still Allows Satan

You must remember this; the devil is a defeated foe, only permitted to be around ultimately to serve God's purpose, when he thinks he is destroying us. We are not to give him room in our lives. We are to resist him and he will flee from us. We can enjoy total victory over Satan and his cohorts right now on earth. And very soon, God shall cause an angel to put him in chains and banish him from the earth for ever.

And the God of peace shall bruise Satan under your feet shortly. The grace of our Lord Jesus Christ be with you. Amen.   Romans 16:20

Chapter Thirteen

Victory Over The Devil

It is possible to have victory over the devil and live in it. The devil has been put under the feet of Jesus Christ. Christ is the Head of the Church, we are His body, His feet. Hence the devil has been put under us, and it is possible to keep him permanently under not allowing him to overcome us at all.

Submit Yourself To God

The first step into this victory is for you to submit yourself to God.

> *Submit yourselves, therefore, to God. Resist the devil, and he will flee from you.*   James 4:7

The devil is a supernatural being. There is no single man in the world that can overcome the devil in his own strength. But God in us gives us the victory by faith. Hence we are to submit ourselves fully to God and then resist the devil.

Some people have not submitted themselves to God at all. They have not been born again. Trying to resist the devil they find him putting them into greater bondage.

The seven sons of Sceva tried it, wanting to cast out devils without having first submitted themselves to God. The devil overcame them and treated them mercilessly, Acts 19:14–16. Give yourself over to God. Let Christ come to live in your heart and He will overcome the enemy through you.

Some saints are not fully yielded to the Holy Spirit. They still struggle in the energy of the flesh and use their own reasoning to work things out. We do not overcome the devil by might or by power. It is by the Spirit of God. You cannot know true victory unless you are fully yielded to God and allow the Holy Spirit to work in and through you.

Be Filled With The Spirit

Secondly, you have to be filled with the Holy Spirit. This is spiritual warfare and it is the Holy Spirit alone that can enable us. That is why God ordained that apart from being born again we should be baptised in the Holy Spirit, endued with power from on high.

Have you received the Holy Spirit since you believed? Have you been baptised, with the initial experience of speaking with tongues? Is the power of God a living reality in your life? If not, you should seek the Lord, pray and receive the fullness of the Spirit which He has promised you by faith. *'For the promise is unto you, and to your children, and to all that are afar off, even as many as the Lord our God, shall call'* Acts 2:39.

And there are some Christians who although they have been baptised in the Holy Spirit are not showing forth the power of God in their lives. We are to be constantly filled with the Spirit, constantly manifesting the power and the glory of God. Do not depend on past anointing. The anointing of the Holy Spirit upon you must be fresh every day. Be filled with the Spirit.

Watch And Pray

Thirdly, to have victory over the devil we have to watch and pray. Many of us are not sober-minded. Many of us are not watchful. Many of us are too loose, too relaxed, to the extent that we are not prayerful. What ails us? Have we not read in the Bible that we should watch and pray lest we enter into temptation? Was it not Jesus Christ our Lord Himself who said it? Have we not read that we should *'be sober, be vigilant: because your adversary the devil, as a roaring lion, walketh about, seeking whom he may devour'* 1 Peter 5:8? Don't we know that because the end of all things is at hand we have to be sober and watchful and prayerful? Cast frivolity aside. Cast laxity aside. Control your tongue from excessive talking and foolish jesting. Mean business like people who are at war. Overcome the enemy by watching and praying.

Give Him No Place

Fourthly, the Bible says: *'Neither give place to the devil'* Ephesians 4:27. Do not allow the devil a foothold. He may come and whisper something hoping to paint it in your heart. Do not give him room. Pluck off all his words by the Word of God and destroy them.

This verse of the scripture can also be quoted as meaning that we should not give the devil any chance to tempt us. A man of God said that many people tempt the devil to tempt them. Is it not true that

Victory Over The Devil

many unnecessarily expose themselves to temptations by their acts and deeds? Let us not deliberately open a way for the devil to tempt us. The devil is very cunning. He exploits situations to launch an attack. He comes around to tempt at unexpected times, using unexpected situations and probably through unexpected persons.

You might have just won a spiritual battle or had a victory. You might have just done an exploit for the Lord. At such a time when you are rejoicing in victory and making your boast in the Lord, watch out and be prayerful.

Do not take anything or any person for granted. This is because the devil can use unexpected situations to launch an attack and he can come subtly through somebody you least expect he can use. This is not for you to go about suspecting people but for you to watch and pray, and not to open an avenue for the devil even ignorantly.

In addition to this, know your weak points and guard them jealously so that the enemy does not take an advantage of them. This is wisdom. Some people do not take notice of this, the devil takes advantage of them and hits them hard.

This is the foolishness of Solomon in spite of his wisdom. This is the weakness of Samson in spite of his might. Let us not fall into the same mistake. Know what can easily lead to sin and avoid it carefully. Flee the appearance of sin. The story was told of Billy Graham, the world renowned evangelist, that he does not allow any lady to be unnecessarily close to him other than his wife. No wonder he keeps going strong. He has high moral principles. Many thought they were strong. They went on carelessly, in foolishness, and stumbled. *'Let him that thinks he stands take heed lest he fall'* 1 Corinthians 10:12.

Resist The Devil

Another point is that you must resist the devil. Stand against him. Do not allow him to have his way. Stand in his way. Challenge him using your authority. Command him. '. . . *Resist the devil and he will flee from you*' James 4:7. The devil is a coward. When he discovers that a child of God knows his right he takes to his heels. Do not think there will not be temptations. Do not think the devil will not challenge. He surely will. But greater is He that is in you than the devil that is in the world. Resist him steadfastly and be an overcomer.

This applies whenever the devil wants to bring a sickness to you or to your loved ones, or when he brings temptations or when he wants to hinder God's blessings from reaching you or when he wants to put you in fear. Resist the devil. He will flee.

Stand Your Ground

Lastly, stand your ground for God. Do not allow the enemy to dispossess you. He is a thief. He will want to steal the blessings God has given. Stand your ground and do not allow him to. Hold fast to your confession of faith. Some people, after receiving healing allow the devil to take the healing away. Some, after receiving a blessing, allow the devil to corrupt or pervert it. Do not allow the enemy into the inheritance God has given you.

This is also applicable to waiting on the Lord for a blessing. You believe God for something. You ask Him in prayer according to His Word. Then you wait for the manifestation. The Word says: *'Therefore I say to you, whatever things you ask when you pray, believe that you receive them, and you will have them'* Mark 11:24 NKJV. You have desired. You have asked. You have believed that you have received. Wait, and you shall have it. The devil will want you to doubt and lose your conviction. Do not listen to Him. Hold fast your confession of faith for faithful is He that has promised. He will do it.

Contend With Him In Battle

God does not want His Church to be playing the defensive. He wants us to move forward and assault the gates of hell. And the gates of hell will not be able to withstand. They will crumble.

That is what Jesus Christ meant when He said *'I will build my church, and the gates of hell shall not prevail against it'* Matthew 16:18.

God needs men and women who are genuinely born again, fully delivered from every bondage of the enemy, thoroughly baptised in the Holy Spirit and who are living a life of total obedience to the Holy Spirit. With these men and women He wants to attack the gates of hell and win the battle. He shall equip these people with various gifts and callings and ministries, and send them around the world like flames of fire. Some of them shall do nothing apart from preaching the Word. These are few. The majority shall use their various jobs and daily work as opportunities to show forth the glory and power of God who has called them out of darkness into his marvellous light; and God shall use these men and women mightily to the glory of His name.

As for you, what are you doing now? Do you meet the requirements stated above? If not, you can, right now. God has no need of useless, self-satisfied Christians who are not ready to move forward. Arise and begin to contend with the devil in battle. Men and women in the world need deliverance. Millions need the Gospel. It is you the Lord wants to use. The devil cannot stand you. You are more than a conqueror. Hear the word of God:

Rise ye up, take your journey, and pass over the river Arnon; behold, I have given into thine hand Sihon, the Amorite, king of Heshbon, and his land. Begin to possess it, and contend with him in battle.   Deuteronomy 2:24

Therefore begin to use your weapons of war and begin to overcome the devil. You are not alone. The Lord is with you. He is your strength.

Behold, I give unto you power to tread on serpents and scorpions, and over all the power of the enemy; and nothing shall by any means hurt you.   Luke 10:19

Chapter Fourteen

The Overcomers

God has a definite purpose for everyone of His children. There is a reason why He saved us. Therefore if you are born again, thoroughly washed in the blood of Jesus from every filthiness of sin, God has a clear purpose for you.

This purpose is clearly stated in many places in the Bible, the Word of God.

> *And we know that all things work together for good to them that love God, to them who are the called according to his purpose.*
>
> *For whom he did foreknow, he also did predestinate to be conformed to the image of his Son, that he might be the firstborn among many brethren.*
>
> *Moreover, whom he did predestinate, them he also called; and whom he called, them he also justified; and whom he justified, them he also glorified.* Romans 8:28–30

You can see the process by which God saved each of His children. It cost Him the precious blood of Jesus Christ His Son. Our salvation actually cost Him much. But above that, you can see His ultimate purpose in doing all He did – THAT WE MIGHT BE CONFORMED TO

THE IMAGE OF HIS SON, THAT WE MIGHT BE GLORIFIED WITH JESUS.

Now get it straight. God did not save you just for church services, fellowships and retreats and conferences. All these are very good. He did not save you to remain a baby Christian. He saved you so that you might grow and mature spiritually, to overcome all problems and hindrances that stand in your way, to fulfil the work He has committed to you on earth and to enter into glory as an overcomer. Blessed be the name of the Lord!

In John 17:24, the Lord Jesus was praying to the Father on our behalf, saying: *'Father, I will that they also, whom thou hast given me, be with me where I am, that they may behold my glory, which thou hast given me; for thou lovedst me before the foundation of the world.'*

The Bible further says that it is in order to bring *'many sons unto glory'* that Jesus suffered the way He did (Hebrews 2:10).

The apostle John, describing what will happen to the saints at the coming of Christ said: *'Beloved, now are we the sons of God, and it doth not yet appear what we shall be, but we know that, when he shall appear, we shall be like him; for we shall see him as he is'* 1 John 3:2.

Jesus Christ our Lord again, appearing to John on the Island of Patmos, re-stated God's ultimate purpose for us:

To him that overcometh will I grant to sit with me in my throne, even as I also overcame, and am set down with my Father in His throne. Revelation 3:21

To enter into eternal glory, to be like the Lord Jesus Christ, to sit with Christ on His throne and to reign, is the ultimate goal of God for every born again Christian.

It seems so great and unimaginable, yet it is true because God said it in His Word.

The devil knows this to be true. That is why he is fighting desperately to hinder the child of God from going forward, or to cause him to fall aside.

To be an overcomer is to overcome all the devices of the devil, the flesh and the world and to fight the good fight of faith in this world, finish your Christian race successfully here and ultimately enter into eternal glory.

It is good to emphasise here that this is the will of God for you. He has done everything needed to make it possible, and He is making 'all things', all events and every creature, work together to accomplish this purpose in you as His child (Romans 8:28). He only needs your co-operation in terms of faith and obedience. There is nothing to be done that is left undone. He has set the stage for you!

Great War Going On

There is a great war in which the Christian is engaged. There is serious opposition of the flesh, tremendous pressure from the world and terrible hostility of the devil and his cohorts to ensure that we come short of the perfect will of God. A child of God who will be an overcomer must overcome in all of these three realms: the flesh, the world and the devil.

We have to fight the good fight of faith. We have to keep trusting and obeying. We are overcomers – more than conquerors through Christ. Do not mind the afflictions or whatever it costs to uphold the victory Christ has given you. Your present afflictions cannot be compared with the glory that shall be shown in us for eternity. God is with us. Glory be to His name!

It is not everybody that shall be an overcomer. No. Not everybody that goes to church or calls on the name of Jesus Christ. I want to say this loud and clear that you may examine yourself whether you are in the company of the overcomers or not. Jesus Christ the Lord said:

> *Not everyone that saith unto me, Lord, Lord, shall enter into the kingdom of heaven, but he that doeth the will of my Father, who is in heaven.*
>
> *Many will say to me in that day, Lord, Lord, have we not prophesied in thy name? And in thy name have cast out devils? And in thy name done many wonderful works?*
>
> *And then will I profess unto them, I never knew you; depart from me, ye that work iniquity.*
>
> Matthew 7:21–23

Prophecies and miracles are very good. They are given by God and they bless and edify us. But the fact that you prophesy, see visions, dream dreams or do miracles in the name of Christ does not imply that you are in the company of the overcomers. You have to depart from iniquity. You have to do the will of God, for, *'the foundation of God standeth sure, having this seal, The Lord knoweth them that are his; and, Let every one that nameth the name of Christ depart from iniquity'* 2 Timothy 2:19.

In the same manner, the fact that you are born again does not mean you are in the company of the overcomers. Jesus said, *'He that shall endure to the end, the same sha⁻¹ be saved'* Matthew 24:13. In His messages to the churches in Revelation 2 and 3, He gave

The Overcomers

several warnings that we should take time to overcome. He gave promises to those who will overcome. There are several other warnings in the Scripture. This is one of them:

> *Behold, I come quickly; hold that fast which thou hast, that no man take thy crown.* Revelation 3:11

If it were automatic for everybody to be an overcomer, there would be no need for such repeated warnings, or any call to avoid the danger of losing the crown. But he knows that even among those who claim to be born again, one time or the other some will fall aside, some will turn away from the faith, some will fall to one snare of the devil or the other. This is not to scare you but to challenge you to make up your mind to be an overcomer. Even if people fall daily, the grace of God shall see you through.

Chapter Fifteen

Character Of The Overcomers

Having made up your mind to be an overcomer, let us examine the character of the overcomers. There are certain qualities peculiar to them. This is to make you understand what is expected of you as an overcomer and to adjust your life to measure up to that standard. The Lord will give you a touch of grace.

Total Surrender

The first striking characteristic of the overcomers is that they are fully surrendered to the Lord Jesus Christ. They are real disciples. They have fully yielded themselves to the Lord. He is not only a Saviour to them but Lord as well. They desire nothing but His perfect will in every aspect of their lives. You know there is the permissive, the acceptable, the good and the perfect will of God. These people (overcomers) want nothing but His perfect will in every sphere of their lives – whether in the choice of a life partner, or in their relationship at home as a family, in the work they do or where they work, in their finances and budgeting, or in giving to the work of the Lord, in serving the Lord with all their hearts, or responding to the call of the ministry. In everything, they are fully given over to Jesus. He is their Lord, and they have made up their minds to steadfastly continue in His Word, in faith, obedience, and love.

So likewise, whoever of you does not forsake all that he has cannot be My disciple. Luke 14:33 NKJV

This is not to say you should abandon your material possessions. It simply means you should turn over the control of all you have and all you shall ever be to Jesus Christ that He might be the sole Controller and Lord of your life. Then you will decide to continue steadfastly in His Word.

Then said Jesus to those Jews who believed on him, If ye continue in my word, then are ye my disciples indeed. John 8:31

When you sincerely and decidedly surrender all you are or have or shall have or be and the whole plan of your life to Jesus Christ, in a quality decision, you have taken the first step into being an overcomer.

Fully Committed

The second striking fact about overcomers is that they are fully committed to the cause of Christ on earth, even to the point of death.

Jesus Christ the LORD is the number one Overcomer. He overcame the devil, the world, the flesh, death, the grave and all foes. We follow in His steps in this victory.

But how and why did He overcome? It was because

He was fully committed to the cause of the Father, seeking nothing but the Father's perfect will, even to the point of death. He said:

My food is to do the will of Him who sent Me, and to finish His work.   John 4:34 NKJV

If we will overcome, we must be fully committed to the cause of Christ on earth. We must do our utmost for His highest, so that His Kingdom will be established in the hearts of men, and His will be done on earth as it is in heaven. You may not have to quit your job and become a pastor or an evangelist – ever. Whatever your field of employment is, the dominating factor should be establishing the Lordship of Jesus. Let the people know He is Lord. He must reign until all His enemies are made His footstool.

This will take your time, your money, your leisure, your life and it might invite some degree of persecution. Yet the overcomers do not love their lives to death. They are ready to spend and be spent for the cause of Christ. They are ready to suffer persecution (from friends, relations, co-workers, bosses) and to shed their blood if the need arises. About the overcomers the Bible says:

And they overcame him by the blood of the Lamb, and by the word of their testimony; and they loved not their lives unto the death.   Revelation 12:11

Do not be half-hearted in your commitment to Christ and his cause on earth. Do not try to be a secret disciple, a silent and fearful Christian. Do not try to save your own life. You cannot be an overcomer that way. Jesus

Christ said: *'For whosoever will save his life shall lose it.'* Luke 9:24.

Daring And Bold

The third characteristic of the overcomers is that they are very daring and bold in Christ. Inasmuch as they are in the will of God for their lives, they refuse to be moved by whatever may be the consequences: they go into it with utter boldness, trusting in the grace of God. Menpleasers cannot be overcomers. The overcomers do not compromise the will of God at all. They stand their ground and are bold in doing so. Such were Meshach, Shadrach and Abednego. They were strangers in Babylon. The king commanded them to worship a golden image. They knew it was not God's will for them to do so. They stood by that decision even when they were threatened with a fiery furnace.

> *Shadrach, Meshach, and Abednego, answered and said to the king, O Nebuchadnezzar, we are not careful to answer thee in this matter.*
>
> *If it be so, our God, whom we serve, is able to deliver us from the burning fiery furnace, and he will deliver us out of thine hand, O king.*
>
> *But if not, be it known unto thee, O king, that we will not serve thy gods, nor worship the golden image which thou hast set up.*   Daniel 3:16–18

They told the king that God was able to deliver them out of his hands, but even if God decided not to deliver them they were not going to worship his idols. That is the faith of an overcomer. They were not refusing to worship idols simply because they knew the Lord would rescue them. They were prepared to face whatever may be the consequences, and rather be consumed in fire in obeying the living God than to live and deny Him. Many of us obey God and do His will just because of the blessings that will follow, or to secure deliverance from the Lord. The overcomer will obey God and do His will not just because of the blessings and deliverances he will get, but because of his regard to the Sovereignty and Lordship of Jesus Christ, who is to be pleased in all things. Let that be the reason for your obedience.

Warriors Of Faith

The overcomers could be very violent. This is another characteristic feature of overcomers. They take a firm decision on the will of God and resist anything contrary. They deal violently with all things that seem to oppose the will of God.

This is not physical violence, but spiritual violence. It is using the weapons of our warfare to deal with the devil.

Remember the Lord Jesus said *'From the days of John the Baptist until now the kingdom of heaven suffereth violence, and the violent take it by force'* Matthew 11:12. Remember that when the Lord was commissioning Jeremiah the prophet, He said:

> *See, I have this day set thee over the nations and over the kingdoms, to root out, and to pull down, and to destroy, and to throw down, to build, and to plant.*   Jeremiah 1:10

What else could this mean but violence – to use the Word of God verbally to deal with the devil and destroy

Character Of The Overcomers

all his works and to bring the will of God to pass. In casting out demons, in healing the sick, in resisting the devil we have to be violent spiritually. We must enforce the victory of Calvary and establish the Lordship of Jesus Christ. He said:

> *Go ye into all the world, and preach the gospel to every creature.*
> *He that believeth and is baptized shall be saved; but he that believeth not shall be damned.*
> *And these signs shall follow those who believe: In my name shall they cast out devils; they shall speak with new tongues;*
> *They shall take up serpents; and if they drink any deadly thing, it shall not hurt them; they shall lay hands on the sick, and they shall recover.*
> Mark 16:15–18

That is nothing but spiritual violence.

The devil may lay a siege against you. He may want to bring sickness to you. He may want to put a mountain in your way. He may even be blocking your way to success and prosperity. You don't fold your arms and keep looking. Resist him violently! Use your weapons of warfare that

> *are not carnal, but mighty through God to the pulling down of strongholds,*
> *Casting down imaginations, and every high thing that exalteth itself against the knowledge of God, and bringing into captivity every thought to the obedience of Christ;*
> *And having in a readiness to avenge all disobedience, when your obedience is fulfilled*
> 2 Corinthians 10:4–5

That is the way to be an overcomer. Overcomers in essence, are warriors of righteousness.

Never Discouraged

The last characteristic of overcomers that we want to examine is that they are NEVER discouraged.

A Christian who is easily discouraged cannot amount to anything for God. Many wonderful ventures have been abandoned because the people met with problems and obstacles and were discouraged. Many of the children of Israel could not enter into the promised land because they were discouraged along the way. Discouragement will make you fall short of the will of God. Discouragement will hinder you from being an overcomer. Refuse to be discouraged. It is not of God. It is a negative spiritual force. Overcome evil with good.

Discouragement can take various forms. Many get discouraged because they accidentally fall into sin and stumble. This is why the devil brings about temptations to sin. You need not be discouraged at all. All you need to do is to confess your sins, renew your allegiance to the Lord Jesus and begin to walk in victory. The Bible says *'If we confess our sins, he is faithful and just to forgive us our sins, and to cleanse us from all unrighteousness'* 1 John 1:9.

Many are discouraged because of persecutions and pressures. Discouragement can come as a result of needs that are not yet met or prayers that are not yet answered. I have seen people get discouraged because they have not found their life partner; others because they have not gained admission into higher institutions; some because they have not got one need or the other met. Some men of God even get discouraged

Character Of The Overcomers

because of lack of finances or lack of fruit of their labour. Never be discouraged. Keep trusting the Lord and then you shall be an overcomer.

> *Cast not away, therefore, your confidence, which hath great recompense of reward.*
>
> *For ye have need of patience that, after ye have done the will of God, ye might receive the promise.* Hebrews 10:35-36
>
> *But, beloved, we are persuaded better things of you, and things that accompany salvation, though we thus speak.*
>
> *For God is not unrighteous to forget your work and labour of love, which ye have showed toward his name, in that ye have ministered to the saints, and do minister.*
>
> *And we desire that every one of you do show the same diligence to the full assurance of hope unto the end;*
>
> *That ye be not slothful, but followers of them who through faith and patience inherit the promises.*
> Hebrews 6:9-12

There are manifold promises available to us as we overcome. Do not be discouraged. Enter into the promises and walk in the benefits of an overcoming life.

Let us learn from the communists. Before they took China over, it was tough for them. In snow, on mountains, in caves, they prepared and trained themselves. When they fought the ruling king, they were beaten severely. Many of them were killed. But the few that were left went to war again. They tried on several occasions and succeeded at last. **The quitter does not win; the winner does not quit**. Do not be discouraged, be an overcomer. And if you have stumbled along the way, rise and take courage again. The Lord is still with you and He still loves you. You can be an overcomer if you do not cast off your confidence.

The steps of a good man are ordered by the LORD, and he delighteth in his way.
Though he fall, he shall not be utterly cast down; for the LORD upholdeth him with his hand.
Psalm 37:23–24

Chapter Sixteen
Being An Overcomer

You overcome by using the weapon of your warfare in fighting the good fight of faith. Do not fold your arms and expect things to be very easy. *'Fight the good fight of faith.'* Do not allow the devil to do anything he likes with you. Resist the devil and he will flee from you. **There is no crown without a cross; there is no victory without a struggle**. The difference with us (children of God) is that ours is a fight of faith, and we use spiritual weapons.

God has provided us with certain weapons which we can use to overcome the enemy. These weapons are mighty and dynamic in their workings, they are irresistible in their applications, they are effectual and can never fail when rightly applied.

We have the name of Jesus – the name that heaven and earth and all obey. When used in faith it releases tremendous spiritual force. We have the Word of God, the same Word with which He spoke the universe into existence. It has not lost its creative power. The Word of God on the lips of faith is like God speaking. It is the sword of the Spirit by which we slay all opposing forces of darkness. We can boldly enter into the presence of God and claim all we need – grace and mercy and provision – to succeed. Jesus said that if we ask anything in His name He will do it. That is the unlimited scope of prayer. *'The effectual, fervent prayer of a righteous man availeth much'* James 5:16. We also have anointing and gifts of the Holy Spirit, giving us supernatural equipment for this battle. We have the weapon of praise – the mightiest of them all and by God's ordained sincere fasting, we can effectively put to use all of these weapons when occasion demands it.

God has made adequate provision for our victory. Let us learn to know what He has provided. Let us make effective use of them all, and fight the good fight of faith. Dare to be an overcomer.

Some saints have been in this battle before us. The devil violently opposed them. But they obtained a good report. They overcame.

> *And they overcame him by the blood of the Lamb, and by the word of their testimony; and they loved not their lives unto the death.* Revelation 12:11

You see how they overcame?

By the blood of the Lamb. No single human being can overcome the devil in his own strength. But there is a Lamb that was slain whose blood thrust out the devil from his stronghold and paralysed him. That Lamb is Jesus Christ. He prevailed. He won the battle. Because He won, we can win. His blood is still the mark of our victory. When the devil sees that blood on us, he flees; all his devices are rendered impotent, because we are covered with the blood of Jesus.

You may look at the enemy and think the battle is hopeless. You may look at your problems and suppose there is no way out. You may have burdens and pressures so great that you begin to weep, lamenting as if there is no hope.

Being An Overcomer

> *'Weep not; behold, the Lion of the tribe of Judah,*
> *. . . hath prevailed.*   Revelation 5:5

He prevailed for you personally. We are not following after fables. Jesus has literally won the victory; by the blood we can and shall overcome.

They overcame by the word of their testimony. The word of faith that proceeded out of their mouths gave them the victory. The devil tried to lay sickness on them. They spoke the word and had their healing. You can use the word of faith in your mouth to win in every situation. Confess positively. Let your confession agree with the Word of God. Make a bold claim on the promises of God. Your word of faith is your sword for battle. It can be a flaming sword if you are filled with the Spirit. Use the Word effectively and be an overcomer.

> *But what saith it? The word is nigh thee, even in thy mouth, and in thy heart that is, the word of faith, which we preach:*
>
> *That if thou shalt confess with thy mouth the Lord Jesus, and shalt believe in thine heart that God hath raised him from the dead, thou shalt be saved.*
>
> *For with the heart man believeth unto righteousness; and with the mouth confession is made unto salvation.*   Romans 10:8–10

They did not love their lives unto death. This is the secret of overcoming. They gave themselves fully into this battle of Life.

Esther said, *'if I perish, I perish'* Esther 4:16. The three Hebrew children said that even if God did not deliver them they were ready to go into the furnace of fire (Daniel 3:17-18). Paul said he was ready not only to suffer for the sake of Christ, but also to die (Acts 21:13).

This is the general attitude of the overcomers. They are ready to suffer anything so that God will be glorified. Make up your mind also. Be committed enough as not to love your life unto the death. Jesus Christ said,

> *Whosoever will save his life shall lose it; but whosoever shall lose his life for my sake and the gospel's, the same shall save it . . .*
>
> *except a seed of wheat fall into the ground and die, it abideth alone; but if it die, it bringeth forth much fruit.* Mark 8:35; John 12:24

Your commitment on this issue should be total and final, knowing that whoever puts his hands on the plough yet looks back is not fit for the Kingdom of God (Luke 9:62). Make a quality decision to stand your ground. Love not your life unto the death.

In this fight of faith, we should put in our best as if all depends on us, yet absolutely trusting in the living God by whom we have the victory. We should never think we are so spiritual that we can make it all alone. We should never suppose that our long experience in the Christian race is sufficient. We should always rest on the grace of God and constantly walk to please Him.

It is still very true that *'It is not of him that willeth, nor of him that runneth, but of God that showeth mercy'* Romans 9:16. Let us depend fully on the Lord and always count on His grace.

To overcome, we have to walk by faith. It is by faith we are saved; through grace (Ephesians 2:8). Having been justified by faith, it is by faith we stand

Being An Overcomer

(2 Corinthians 1:24). To succeed, we have to live by faith for the victory that overcomes is faith.

For whatever is born of God overcometh the world; and this is the victory that overcometh the world, even our faith.   1 John 5:4

Do not walk by sight. A spiritual experience based on feelings is unreliable. Your prayer life, your witnessing, your living generally should be based upon the principles of the Word of God. Walk by faith and not by sight. Christ has won the victory for us; when you walk by faith, you enter and dwell in this victory and the devil cannot do anything about it.

Overcoming In Every Area

You have to overcome in every aspect of your life. In the area of honesty and integrity, you should be an overcomer. As far as temptations and sins are concerned you should be an overcomer. Over the lusts of the flesh, the enticement of the world as well as over the pressures the devil may mount against you, you should be an overcomer. At work, at home, in the family, at school, in persecution, you should overcome. Jesus Christ the Lord said this about the church of which you are a member:

I will build my church, and the gates of hell shall not prevail against it.   Matthew 16:18

Since the host of hell cannot prevail against the church they cannot prevail against you. Paul the apostle said:

Who shall separate us from the love of Christ? Shall tribulation, or distress, or persecution, or famine, or nakedness, or peril, or sword?

As it is written, For thy sake we are killed all the day long; we are accounted as sheep for the slaughter.

Nay, in all these things we are more than conquerors through him that loved us.

For I am persuaded that neither death, nor life, nor angels, nor principalities, nor powers, nor things present, nor things to come,

Nor height, nor depth, nor any other creature, shall be able to separate us from the love of God, which is in Christ Jesus, our Lord. Romans 8:35–39

This is an overcomer's mentality in every aspect of his life. Develop this mentality and adopt this attitude.

Chapter Seventeen

God's Promises To The Overcomers

There are many promises for the overcomers. Remember, God is faithful. What He says, He will do. All His promises are yea and amen in Christ Jesus. The Lord Jesus said: *'He that shall endure unto the end, the same shall be saved'* Matthew 24:13. This is talking about our ultimate deliverance from this present world to enter into the glory God has prepared for us. This is for the overcomers alone. Those who fall by the wayside or who give in to pressures and difficulties and abandon the faith have no part in it. Therefore, be an overcomer, endure to the end.

Indescribable Glory

Paul the apostle said,

For our light affliction which is but for a moment, worketh for us a far more exceeding and eternal weight of glory;

For I reckon that the sufferings of this present time are not worthy to be compared with the glory which shall be revealed in us.

2 Corinthians 4:17; Romans 8:18

Jesus is coming to be glorified in us. The great glory that shall be revealed in the overcomers cannot be described in words.

Sometime ago I watched a Christian film called *The Believers' Heaven*. The scene described was charming. Yet what is prepared for the overcomer is greater than what eyes have seen or ears have heard. That is what is prepared for you.

Jesus, sending messages to the seven Asian churches as recorded in Revelation chapters two to three, made some promises to the overcomers.

Eating Of The Tree of Life

> *To him that overcometh will I give to eat of the tree of life, which is in the midst of the paradise of God.*
> Revelation 2:7

Adam and Eve lost access to this tree when they were driven from God's presence because of their sin. Anyone who has been justified in Christ, who overcomes, at last will eat of the fruit of this tree of life. What this means fully I cannot now explain. When we get there and we are doing the eating, we shall understand. But I perceive this tree of life shall make us live for endless days in the presence of the living God. Glory!

> *To him that overcometh will I give to eat of the hidden manna, and will give him a white stone, and in the stone a new name written, which no man knoweth saving he that receiveth it.*
> Revelation 2:17

There will be a lot of excitement and wonder for the overcomers. There will be deep satisfaction and

God's Promises To The Overcomers

fulfilment as we eat of the hidden manna and receive the white stone with the new name. It pays to remain forever a faithful soldier of Christ; every sacrifice made in His name shall have its rich and full compensation.

Never To Die Again

He that overcometh shall not be hurt of the second death. Revelation 2:11

The Bible talks of three kinds of death. There is the spiritual death, which means separation from God, partaking of the sin nature and being under the dominion of sins. This is the state of every man that is not born again. There is the physical death – the separation of the body from spirit and soul. There is the eternal death, otherwise known as the second death. This is the state of any human being who dies without accepting Jesus as his Lord and Saviour. He is lost for ever.

As an overcomer, when you accepted Jesus as Lord and Saviour, you passed from death into life. The devil tries everything to draw you back to the position of death but you overcome through the grace of God. You will live with God for ever. You will not have part in the lake of fire, which is the second death. *'Because I live,'* Jesus said, *'ye shall live also.'* Glory be to the Lord.

He that overcometh, and keepeth my works unto the end, to him will I give power over the nations;
And he shall rule them with a rod of iron; as the vessels of a potter shall they be broken to shivers, even as I received of my Father.
And I will give him the morning star.
Revelation 2:26–28

There are exciting promises here. Jesus is coming back to rule the earth for one thousand years. Bible scholars call it 'The Millennium'. The overcomers shall come to reign with Him. They will rule over nations with power and authority; in righteousness and purity. The morning star is associated with the millennial reign of Christ. We shall have the morning star. Alleluia.

> *He that overcometh, the same shall be clothed in white raiment; and I will not blot out his name out of the book of life, but I will confess his name before my Father, and before his angels.* Revelation 3:5

There are people who do not bother about holiness and righteousness. Their nakedness shall be seen on the day of judgement. There are those whose names are not written in the Lamb's book of life, they shall be cast into the lake of fire. They shall be tormented for ever. There are cowards who are ashamed to confess the name of Jesus Christ before their friends, parents and relatives; Jesus will not confess their names before the Father and His angels, they have no part with Him.

The overcomers are not so. They follow after righteousness, holiness, purity and integrity. They will be clothed with white raiment and not be found naked. They have been born again by receiving Jesus as their Saviour and Lord; their names are in the Book of Life. They are never ashamed of Jesus. They confess His name in spite of persecution; and because they suffer with Him they shall reign with Him.

> *Him that overcometh will I make a pillar in the temple of my God, and he shall go no more out; and I will write upon him the name of my God, and the name of the city of my God, the new Jerusalem,*

> *which cometh down out of heaven from my God; and I will write upon him my new name.*
>
> Revelation 3:12

You will become a pillar in the temple of God – immovable, abiding for ever. This is what David had in view when he said, *'Surely goodness and mercy shall follow me all the days of my life and I will dwell in the house of the LORD forever'* Psalm 23:6.

Reigning For Ever And Ever

> *To him that overcometh will I grant to sit with me in my throne, even as I also, overcame, and am set down with my Father in his throne.*
>
> Revelation 3:21

To share the throne with Christ is the final stage of our exaltation as His Body. His Bride. Now we are exercising authority over the devil and his cohorts. Then, we shall literally reign with Him over the universe. This actually proves that all things are for the overcomer. *'And so shall we ever be with the Lord'* 1 Thessalonians 4:17.

> *He that overcometh shall inherit all things, and I will be his God, and he shall be my son.*
>
> Revelation 21:7

Chapter Eighteen
He That Hath An Ear . . .

If you open your Bible and take a close look at the passage where these promises are given, you will see that they are closely linked with a particular phrase:

He that hath an ear, let him hear what the Spirit saith unto the churches.   Revelation 2:29

There are many voices clamouring for our attention today. But this is what the Spirit is saying to the churches. God wants the Church to be strong. He wants the saints to be overcomers. Jesus Christ is not coming for a weak, discouraged and defeated set of people begging for deliverance. He is coming for a people that are holy and pure, strong and energetic, daring and bold, who are making demons submit and the world to tremble because Jesus Christ is Lord. You can be in that company. The Lord has given wonderful promises to those who overcome. The promises are for you.

If you have been born again, hear this word of God *'Thou therefore, my son, be strong in the grace that is in Christ Jesus. . . . Be strong in the Lord and in the power of his might . . . Fight the good fight of faith, lay hold on eternal life . . .'* Be thou an overcomer. 2 Timothy 2:1; Ephesians 6:10; 1 Timothy 6:12.

Paul was an example. He heard the call of God and obeyed immediately. He gave himself fully to the service of Jesus the Lord. He fought a good fight and entered into glory. He was an overcomer. Therefore he could say:

I have fought a good fight, I have finished my course, I have kept the faith;
  Henceforth, there is laid up for me a crown of righteousness, which the Lord, the righteous judge, shall give me at that day; and not to me only, but unto all them also that love his appearing.
  Do thy diligence to come shortly unto me.
  2 Timothy 4:7–9

He fought the good fight. He finished his course. He kept the faith. He was expecting a crown. He then gave an exhortation: *Do your diligence, your best to be an overcomer like me. Fight the good fight. Finish your course. Keep the faith. Then enter into glory, an overcomer.*

If you have not been born again there is still room for you at the cross of Christ. You can then become an overcomer. Simply repent of your sins and give yourself fully to Jesus Christ as your Saviour and Lord. He will save you. He will make you an overcomer. Do it now.

JESUS IS LORD!

The Sword of the Spirit Teaching Paper

To receive a regular bi-monthly teaching of God's Word, news about the ministry of Rev Francis Wale Oke and the Sword of the Spirit Ministries, you can subscribe to The Sword of the Spirit, a regular teaching paper of the Sword of the Spirit Ministries. Write to us today at the address given on the last page of this book, and we shall send one to you.

Other Books By Francis Wale Oke

Alone With God
Weapons of Our Warfare
The Power That Works In Us
The Precious Blood of Jesus
Receiving the Power Of The Holy Spirit
Deliverance On Mount Zion
Prevailing Prayers
Possess Your Possession
God's Provision For Your Complete Healing
Go Forward
Victory In Jesus Name
Walking In God's Covenant
Effective Intercession
He Cares For You
Turn To The Rock And Drink
Let Us Pass Over Unto The Other Side

Teaching Tapes (Audio)
By
Francis Wale Oke

Arise And Shine
Absolute Victory
A Change Of Identity
Bringing Down The Glory
The Snare Is Broken
Turn To The Rock And Drink
Let Us Pass Over Unto The Other Side
Is Your Name Written In The Book Of Life?
The Danger Of Compromise
Let The Fire Fall
Walking In God's Covenant
From Curses To Blessing
The Pursuit Of Holiness
Anointing For Wealth
Christian Dressing
Divine Intervention
3-Dimensions Of Warfare
Family Life I, II, III.
Overwelming Anointing.

Teaching Tapes (Video)
By
Francis Wale Oke

Bringing Down the Glory
New Wine For Your Life
Victory by Your Right Hand
The Pursuit Of Holiness
Anointed With Fresh Oil

Overwhelming Anointing
From Curses To Blessings
A New Anointing
The Power To Get Wealth
Walking In God's Covenant
From Glory To Glory
The Glory Of The Latter House
The Blessing Of Abraham
Moving With The Cloud Of Glory
The Foundation For An Effective Ministry
Power In The Word
Let the Fire Fall

Order All Materials From:

Nigeria:
The Sword of the Spirit Ministries
P.O. Box 6308 Agodi P.O.,
Ibadan.
Tel. 234–2–8101473
Telex: 31503 SOTSM NG.

United Kingdom:
The Sword of the Spirit Ministries
P.O. Box 2559,
London NW11 0QQ